WALTZING TO A
DIFFERENT STRUMMER

WALTZING TO A
DIFFERENT STRUMMER

TOM PLUMMER

BOOKCRAFT

SALT LAKE CITY, UTAH

Visit us at www.deseretbook.com

Library of Congress Cataloging-in-Publication Data

Plummer, Tom, 1939-
    Waltzing to a different strummer / Tom Plummer.
        p.   cm.
    ISBN 1-57345-959-3 (pbk.)
    1. Christian life--Mormon authors. I. Title.
    BX8656 .P57 2002
    248.4'89332--dc21   2002001078

Printed in the United States of America   7973-6811
Bang, Brainerd, Minnesota

10   9   8   7   6   5   4   3   2   1

TO MY FOUR SONS

To Jonathan, for teaching me to toughen up

To Ed, for teaching me to lighten up

To Charles, for teaching me to boot up

To Sam, for teaching me to divvy up

CONTENTS

INTRODUCTION

I have written this book in answer to a friend's question. It has been eleven years since he asked it, and he may have forgotten that he ever did. I have not forgotten because it has floated in my brain, drifting in and out of consciousness like a piece of driftwood, for more than a decade.

Sometime in January 1992 I was sitting on the bed in my Provo, Utah, home watching television. Most likely I didn't have energy to do anything else. A few days before, I had emerged from surgery to "debulk" a pituitary tumor that had found a home in the middle of my head. It was too large and dangerous to remove, so surgeons reamed it out like a cantaloupe, nudged it away from the optic nerves, and left the rest of the job to radiation oncologists.

The phone rang. "Hi, Tom, this is Robert." Robert, who was calling from a distant state, has been a friend since the 1960s, when I worked with him in a church assignment. I will always think of Robert as a man of tough questions. When he poses a question, he emphasizes it by raising his

1

right index finger, which he can curve back ever so slightly, and, with eyebrows raised, saying, "This is my question . . ." When Robert raises a question, I just can't ignore him.

He expressed sympathy for my condition and then said, "Well, I have a question."

"Okay," I said. I could imagine his index finger taking its familiar position.

"People say these things change them."

"Yes," I said, "I'm changing my life."

"Well, this is my question," he said. "How do you manage to stay changed?"

"I don't know exactly," I said. "I just know for sure that I'm making changes."

"Yes," he said, "but how do you keep everyday things from dragging you back into your routines?"

"I don't know that right now," I said. "Down inside something's snapped. I've been doing things I really don't want to do. I'm not cut out for them, and I'm not going to do them anymore."

"Yes, for now," he said. "But how do you know you'll be able to make it stick?"

I may not have his words precisely, but his drift was clear. We chatted for a minute or two and then said good-bye. I suspected at the time that Robert was asking the question as much for himself as for me.

I have spent the last ten years gnawing on his question. Not constantly, of course—more like something you've left in the fridge to snack on when you happen to think of it. I have learned some things in the process, things that I imagine many people learn who have taken their cancer, heart attack, or near-fatal accident seriously, things I could not have articulated to Robert that night in my fuzzy state of mind. To be perfectly honest, I am still an ignoramus, a nonexpert, an incompetent; I am writing through a glass darkly.

The short answer to my friend Robert is that I couldn't just stop doing some things and start doing other things, as I originally thought. I've had to reeducate myself; reexamine who I am; reevaluate my values; reconfigure my thinking so that going back to old ways would be inconceivable. It's a process of reverse education in a sense, unlearning the old or salvaging it in new ways; embracing new ideas; redefining what I think is good, true, and beautiful; making life an adventure that is completely my own; putting my gifts to work; risking failure and allowing failure; accepting uncertainty as a fact of life; living each day, each hour fully; reconnecting with ancestors; locating past friends; putting myself in harmony with God and his world; laying anger to rest; and facing my dragons with courage. If there is a theme to all of this, it is striving to become one with God, his children, and his world, and becoming whole with myself, coming to at-one-ment.

My list is far from complete. It's a sampling. I don't know why I had to wait for a crisis to begin my own change, but it took a crisis. I don't know if it takes a crisis for others to change, but I know many who have changed through crisis. I know, sadly, that I had to be staring the end in the face before

I made a new beginning. I'm that stubborn. Abraham Lincoln, in his Second Annual Address to Congress in 1862, said, "The dogmas of the quiet past are inadequate to the stormy present." It took a personal Civil War for me too, Mr. President.

The problem is not so much falling back into old patterns; the problem is sculpting my Self into something I could not have anticipated years ago. The problem is growing up at an advanced age, becoming, always becoming, trying to move toward the person God designed me to be. Erich Fromm called it birth: "The whole life of the individual is nothing but the process of giving birth to himself; indeed we should be fully born when we die" (as quoted in Terry Tempest Williams, *Refuge* [New York: Vintage, 1992], 232).

Achieving birth, achieving completeness, I believe, is a lifelong personal journey. Spouses, friends, and teachers may lend support, may stomp and cheer, but it remains a personal journey. It has to do with learning to treat yourself with love and kindness; with turning away from the things that burn up huge chunks of your life that just aren't going to make a difference. People make a difference. If I can help someone, that's worth the trouble. Friendship makes a difference. My children and grandchildren make a difference. Love makes a difference. God makes all the difference.

The journey to rebirth, to wholeness, to at-one-ment is personal in the same way that love is personal. Marching to someone else's drummer won't cut it. I have reservations about marching. Armies march. Bands march. Marching means uniforms, drum majors, anonymity. Marching is impersonal. The

4

most dangerous thing about marching is getting out of line, becoming personal. Marching is a mass thing. Achieving rebirth is a personal thing. It means listening to one's own rhythms, waltzing to one's own strummer, missing a few steps, finding the beat again. Like it or not, I'm waltzing to a different strummer.

DO YOU JUST LAUGH
ALL THE TIME?

$\mathcal{S}$ometimes people I don't know sidle up and ask, "Do you and your wife just laugh all the time?" Usually this comes after they've read something we've written or heard something we've said. There's a twinge of envy in their voices. And in that moment, I realize that we've misled yet another person. Our public mask has hidden all trace of our private reality.

The fantasy is all too human. We want a fairytale ending. We want to believe that someone, somewhere is leading a perfect life. Just think how angry people would be if Tom Hanks and Meg Ryan didn't get together after all those e-mails or meet on the Empire State Building after all that flying back and forth from Seattle to Manhattan. Everybody hopes there's a perfect life, a perfect child, a perfect friend out there somewhere, even if it's not their own. Hope is even more enduring than the dandelions in my lawn.

Recently I had one of my unpredictable and unsettling panic attacks about money. I can keep it under wraps for as much as two or three days, much longer than in the early years of our marriage, but finally I say something like, "We're going broke tomorrow." And this infects Louise with the same panic, because we are both jittery people. Then I slink around in a funk for a while trying to figure out how to survive, and eventually I say to Louise, "What's on your mind?"

And she says, "Right now I want to jump off a cliff."

Actually, I'm pretty sure she'd like me to jump off a cliff, because I have more life insurance than she has, and she doesn't want to die.

It's clear to me that if we just laughed all the time, we would laugh while we ate, spitting food all over the table; we'd laugh when we brushed our teeth, drooling toothpaste down our chins; and we'd laugh ourselves sick at funerals.

Laughing all the time would *make* us sick. We couldn't have a meaningful conversation. We couldn't pay the bills. We'd dress the children in clown suits. Laugh laugh laugh. We'd die laughing, and if we didn't, we'd have to get divorced. Grounds: Couple say they can't stop laughing, and it is starting to hurt a lot.

"Inverse cripples," the philosopher Friedrich Nietzsche called them: people who get so attached to doing one thing, who are so locked into a routine, so accustomed to using one hand, one foot, one ear that the whole body becomes that one part—a hand or a foot or an eye. I suppose laughers would become all mouth and throat. Nietzsche was writing in the nineteenth century, so he might have added to his list people who spend the day on the computer typing and become all fingers or people whose cell phone replaces their ear.

Sameness, no matter what it is, becomes a tyrant. We become addicted to it, threatened by alternatives and newness. Leaving familiar territory, the trappings of our lives, turns into a frightening exercise. I once assigned my students in Vienna to go to the Art History Museum and sit in front of a painting by Raphael, *The Madonna of the Meadows.* "Examine the painting for at least thirty minutes," I told them. "Look at every part of it. Look at the colors. Look at the composition of the figures. Look at the sky. Look at the earth. How does the painting accomplish its tone? Reflect on your emotions as you look at it. Let it reach deep down inside you. What do you feel? What do you think? Then write a short essay about the experience."

Most of them took to the assignment with enthusiasm. Not Anita. You'd think I had asked her to live in a city of flea-infested rats. "What's so great about a stupid old painting? Why do people like doing things that are so boring? How does Raphael know what those people looked like? Did he have a camera?" Another time I mentioned to her how wonderful Vienna is. "But I love America," she said, as if I were about to burn her passport.

The intensity of her rebellion reflects the degree of her fear. She reminds me of children Louise and I once baby-sat while their parents were away. The children were sweet and obedient, but a single moment from that weekend stands out for me. Louise put the salt and pepper back in the wrong cupboard, and the children began to wail. "Mom doesn't put the salt and pepper there. She puts it over there." Their voices rose with their panic, as if maybe their parents weren't coming home and we were going to be their parents and always put the salt and pepper back in the wrong place.

I used to go fishing with colleagues in northern Minnesota. One guy, Matthew, was absolutely locked into his schedule. Everything was done by the clock, and he became agitated and nervous if things weren't right on time. It became obvious, after two or three days, that 10:00 P.M. was his potty time. He would disappear into the bathroom with a book and remain there for twenty-three minutes every night. It became a joke among the rest of us—just as the hour struck ten, Matthew was gone. It was the same with meals. Dinner had to be at 6:00 P.M., no matter what. If we were out on a stream enjoying the cool evening air, the brilliant red, orange, and yellow of fall in Minnesota, and it looked like we might miss the 6:00 dinner hour, he'd make moves to leave. He'd pack up his gear, start asking if we really thought the fish were going to bite, and on and on. Finally, the rest of us would give up, go back to the cabin, and cook supper.

Just how dedicated he was to this schedule became all too clear one night when we encountered a salmon run, the first of its kind ever in a little stream that fed into Lake Superior. We discovered it quite by accident, wading through the stream at dusk. The water exploded. Fish everywhere. Big fish. We had been catching twelve-inch trout all day, and this was clearly not the same creature. We had no idea what they were, but finally chased one into an eddy where we could shine a flashlight on it and get a look. It was eighteen to twenty inches long, with a thick girth and a humped back. We guessed it was a salmon. We had no idea there were salmon up there. Just then, Matthew began making noises about dinner. It was late. Why didn't we take a look at the situation tomorrow? The rest of us just stared at him with open maws. Could he be serious?

Someone suggested we take him back to the cabin where he could fix himself dinner. The rest of us would return to the stream for a little night fishing. At the cabin we did some quick research. Leafing through one or two books on fish species, we ran across the humpback salmon. At the time of the run, the males develop humps on their backs. Apparently these had escaped their Canadian environs and were making their first run on streams in northern Minnesota via Lake Superior. Now equipped with heavy-duty lanterns and gear we returned to the stream.

The fish were still there. And they weren't taking anything. Not dry flies, not streamers, not worms. Nothing. Ray was standing in a shallow pool casting when he felt something brush against his leg. He shone the light into the water and saw a large salmon just massaging itself against his boot. He reached down quietly and stroked its side. It snuggled into his hand like a kitten. He slid his thumb under its gill and lifted it out of the water with a war cry. But was this legal? He returned the fish to the water, and we read through the Minnesota fishing regulations that Ray had in his bag. No laws against fishing with your hands. None at all. We put our gear aside, rolled up our sleeves, and went into the water with flashlights.

When we returned to the cabin with thirty large salmon that

night, the legal limit, Matthew looked stunned. But only for a moment. "I just had to eat," he said. "I'll give it a try tomorrow."

The next day the salmon were gone.

I read in a magazine once that the Japanese don't follow dietary fads like Americans. Their rule of thumb is this: Eat thirty different foods a day. Now, this could be a serious problem for us in these United States if we're used to having a double cheeseburger, fries, and a Coke for lunch. Even if we break the double cheeseburger into its parts—two slabs of extra-fat hamburger, a leaf of lettuce, two very thin slices of tomato, mustard, mayonnaise, ketchup, and two slices of American almost-cheese—that's seven foods, but let's face it, the two hunks of meat outweigh everything else in sight.

Compare that with a lunch Louise and I bought one day at the train station in Tokyo. In a Japanese train station, you buy a little box lunch. I mean literally a box of lunch—a delicate wooden box with a Japanese design on top, and inside twelve or so little compartments, each with its own tempting food item, prepared with as much attention to beauty as to taste. A miniature banquet. We bought two.

As the train pulled out, we opened our boxes and began. From the first bite I was glad I didn't know what I was eating because it was food with such alien texture and taste, I would never knowingly order it in a restaurant. A little brain, a little ginger root on rice, a little fig of newt, all squares with unfamiliar vegetables and pastries, sometimes rolled together in artful sushi-cylinders. Eating was exhilarating—because I had finally gotten past some hang-ups I've had about exotic foods, and because the net effect was gratifying. I'm glad I did it—and I ate at least twelve of my thirty daily food items.

At fine restaurants, the Japanese turn variety dining into an even higher art than at train stations. Our friend Gordon took us to one, where we had a ten-course meal, if memory serves me correctly. Each course consisted of a marvelously prepared delicacy: fish, quail eggs, mushrooms, braised beef, lamb, and rice pastry. Dishes were served one at a time, and when you were ready to move on, you signaled the waiter, who promptly delivered up the next course. The meal took well over an hour. We left neither hungry nor stuffed. We felt—I find no other words for it—aesthetically and spiritually fed.

By contrast, I heard a news report about a restaurant in Amarillo, Texas, that will serve customers free if they eat a sixty-four-ounce steak in less than an hour. Would-be "winners" sit on a stage at the front of the restaurant, cheered on by other customers and closely observed by steak cops, who ensure that every last bite is eaten. If there's a dispute over whether a hunk of gristle counts as meat, the steak cop decides. Even after finishing, you're not through. You have to wait a full hour to assure the restrepreneurs that you aren't going to throw it all up. One customer ate two meals.

When translated into a lifestyle, the thirty-food diet makes sense to me. A little of this, a little of that, not too much of anything. That way, even though there will always be work I have to do that I don't want to do, I can blend it in with small things that give me pleasure. And I'm more aware that whether the small things are hard or whether they're easy, they're part of my life, the only one I have. I've noticed that the small things, the ones I used to overlook, are really the big things, the ones worth remembering.

What has become important is not the "big" stuff, but the little stuff, with as much variety as I can work in, the small moments that I once overlooked, forgot to savor, never even saw or heard. The small moments when a hummingbird comes up to the feeder, a peony bursts out overnight, a grandchild writes a letter: "Thank you for that thing." It's the message from the Japanese lunch box that I remember—lots of small things are better than one great big thing.

I wouldn't want to laugh all the time. I'd miss out on other little things that mean a lot.

ORGANIC LIVING

Nothing is more deadly to the spirit than an inflexible plan," the Taoist has written. "A good traveler has no fixed plans and is not intent upon arriving. A good artist lets his intuition lead him wherever it wants. A good scientist has freed himself of concepts and keeps his mind open to what is." I have come to think of this attitude as "organic living." Organic, as in the way a tree or flower would grow, not in triangles and squares, not in blocks of time, not with a fixed plan or destination in mind, but by branching out from the root in any number of directions, growing always upward and outward, but in no fully predictable way. Organic living is not always possible in a society that worships day planners, Palm Pilots, and computers that announce the date and time on the screen right in front of us. Still, with a little awareness, organic living can become a large part of each day. Organic living can be as simple as a spontaneous lunch or dinner with someone you meet unexpectedly. It can be as simple as getting an ice cream cone only because you are driving past your favorite 500

14

Flavors joint. It can be as simple as spending unscheduled time on the phone with a son, daughter, or friend. It can be as simple as saying, "I'm going for a ride now to my favorite spot. I'll be back when I get back."

Organic living means finding ways to live intuitively, leaving your schedule open to exploration, meandering, flexibility, and spontaneity. It means sitting quietly and listening deep inside for promptings, moment to moment, rather than planning your work and working your plan. Hush. Listen. Those two words are essential to organic living.

A few years ago, we needed cash. Christmas had passed and left us with our stressed January budget. I decided to move the financial mountain by faith. I prayed for relief. As I sat at my office desk one day, in solitude and silence, a man called who said he represented a motivational company that needed a book translated from German. All of my biases kicked in. Some turkey from a fly-by-night motivational company wants me to put my schedule on hold to translate a book. "How long is it?" I asked.

"About 150 pages," he said.

"And you need it when?" I asked.

"In two weeks at the latest. We have to get this out."

They probably want to pay five dollars a page to translate a book of material that I'm unfamiliar with, I thought, and they want it in two weeks? I didn't have time for this nonsense.

"Well," I said, in my most arrogant voice, "I'm pretty

busy. Maybe we could get together and talk about it some-time."

"I'm afraid we don't have time to talk, Mr. Plummer," he said. "We've got a deadline."

"Well, I'd need to look over the material, to see if it's something I want to do," I said.

"No," he said, "we have to get this done. I'll call someone else."

"Well," I said, "what kind of fee did you have in mind?"

"A local translation firm made a bid of $14,000," he said. "We thought you might do a better job, but we'll move on." He hung up.

I sat stunned and stupid at my desk, where the money I needed had come rolling to my feet. I had been praying for solutions, a man called me out of the blue and offered me a job for two weeks for $14,000, and I snubbed it and got cut off. I called him back.

"Mr. Johnson is in a meeting now," the receptionist said. "May I tell him who's calling?"

I left a message. He never called me back.

I try hard to listen. I try hard to watch for those moments when I should shift into organic living. Sometimes opportunity knocks, enters, and dances around my room, and I still don't see it. I just keep focused on my schedule.

This is an age-old pattern I'm having to overcome. It goes way back to my early years. I was a planning demon. It paid off. I got good grades. I went to good schools. I paid a price. My father, who led a disciplined life, was amazed at how I could out-discipline him. He noticed that when I came home from classes at the university in my college years, I would disappear into my room in the basement and stay there for hours. Once he came downstairs, just out of curiosity, to see if I was sleeping. I was on the books. One day he timed me to see how long it took me to walk through the door and hit the books. Two minutes.

I was so focused when I started dating Louise that I told her we could go out either Friday or Saturday night, but not both. One of the two I had to study. It must have taken some effort on her part not to say, "Why don't you take a flying leap?" But she didn't. She found other solutions. About 9:30 or 10:00 P.M. on any given school night, she would walk the block and a half from her house to mine, go to my basement window, kick on it, and signal that it was time to go for a walk. I would get up and go for a walk with Louise.

The first time this happened, my parents saw me walk out the door. My mother began to fuss. That was Dad's word for Mother's nervous fantasies about pending disasters. She began to fuss. "Gail," she said, "Tom's left the house. He didn't say anything. What do you suppose is wrong?"

She walked out onto the porch. I, of course, was not to be seen. I was out of my cage, walking blissfully with the girl I was going to marry in six months or sooner. Mother looked over the edge of the porch, and there, in the new January snow, were footprints that led directly to my window. Then footprints led away from my window.

Louise and I, in the meantime, finished our walk, smooched a bit, and said goodnight.

As I came up the steps to the house, both of my parents were leaning over the edge of the porch, looking at the footprints in the snow.

"What's going on?" I asked.

"Where have you been?" Mother's voice was half relieved, half scolding.

"I went for a walk with Louise," I said.

"Are those her footprints down there?"

"Yes. She came and kicked on my window, and we went for a walk," I said.

The next day Louise called. Dad answered. "Is Tom there?" she asked.

"Tom who?"

"Tom Plummer."

"Who's this?"

"Louise."

"Oh, the Tom Peeper?"

Louise became the Tom Peeper.

I did not realize then that I was beginning a long journey toward organic living that I could not have understood in those early days of courtship. It was not a natural part of my genetic makeup and certainly not a part of my family heritage.

My mother's family was pioneer stock who settled in Monroe, Sevier County, Utah. Hard labor, farming, was for those people the only means of survival. When my grandparents had two young daughters, my grandfather was called on a mission.

He left his family, furloughed his position as bishop of the Monroe Ward, and rode on a horse-drawn buggy into the northwestern United States for the next two years. My grandmother made ends meet by making and selling ice cream. At age forty-two, my grandfather had a stroke that cost him his leg. How the family—now five children—got along, I do not know. I don't think there was much room for my ideas about organic living.

I began marriage thinking that *work* meant the kind of work my family did. Only slowly did I grow into the realization that Louise's work might be different. I had grown up as an ant, but I had married a grasshopper. In her essay "Thoughts of a Grasshopper," Louise wrote:

> "What about works?" someone may ask. "Don't ants work harder than grasshoppers?"
>
> No. Grasshoppers work *differently* from ants.
>
> I would like to rewrite the ending of "The Grasshopper and the Ants" like this: It is winter, and the grasshopper is walking in the snow, talking to herself and answering herself. She wears a yellow slicker over her sweater, because she can't find her parka (which is buried in the debris under her bed). Because she was out of groceries this morning, she is eating a brownie with a carton of milk bought at the 7-Eleven which, thank heaven, is open 365 days a year. The door in the tree where the ants live swings

open. The queen ant appears and says to the grasshopper, "We are bored to death. Won't you tell us a story or at least a good joke? Our teenagers are driving us crazy; maybe you could write them a play to perform, or just a road show? Do you have any ideas for a daddy-daughter party?"

The grasshopper replies that she has ideas for all of them. So the ant invites her in and seats her at a spotless kitchen table with pencil and paper, and the grasshopper writes the road show.

The ant feeds her guest a slice of homemade bread, fresh from the oven, and a glass of freshly squeezed orange juice. "How do you get all of these ideas?" she asks the grasshopper.

"They come to me," says the grasshopper, "while I am taking long hot baths."

I must have sensed that I needed to marry a grasshopper. Deep down inside I give myself credit for not marrying my duplicate, and I regret the many years when I insisted that she be like me or accept what I was as her own identity.

I needed brain surgery to become a devoted grasshopper. When I was recovering from the operation on my tumor, I wasn't feeling well enough to work hard, so I began insisting that Louise hang out with me. We would go for rides, go to lunch, go for walks, go see friends. Then one day she said in a despairing voice, "You've got to stop this. I *have* to *work*."

"I thought you were a grasshopper," I said.

"I have to *work*," she said.

She was right, of course. Grasshoppers work differently from ants, but they do work. Grasshoppers work and live organically.

Last summer, Louise and I drove back and forth across the country, six thousand miles in all. We had a long break between the two drives, but we decided five hundred miles a day was all we could stand. When I get in this mindset, I go from motel to motel. I prearrange the trip so I know where I'm going to be. This time, Louise convinced me not to get motels in advance. We would drive until we wanted to stop. We stopped in places we wouldn't normally stop, like a Danish town having a Danish celebration. We bought a few souvenirs and some ice cream and moved on.

We stopped in Pella, Iowa, a town founded by the Dutch. Louise, being Dutch, wanted to stop in Pella. It's off the interstate about thirty-five miles, and I, diligently practicing organic living, thought this might be a fine diversion. Pella has fully embraced its Dutch heritage. Buildings in the commercial district have Dutch architecture—brick façades, gables, and, in one mall, a canal. The highlight was a Dutch bakery, where we loaded up on almond pastry to take back to our Dutch motel (at least it had a Dutch souvenir shop) with a half gallon of milk.

Along the way through Iowa, I noticed a sign for another interesting-sounding town, What Cheer. I haven't been to What Cheer, Iowa, yet, but I'll get there. Maybe on the next trip.

SLAYING DRAGONS

The dragon I fight now is the very same dragon I fought forty-five or fifty years ago. It has taken me years to recognize its disguises. During the fights in the ninth-grade locker room after gym class, when Roger, Larry, and Frank were popping each other's hides with wet towels, administering rosy welts the size of Shaquille O'Neal's hands to thighs and derrieres, I would cram myself into a corner and keep quiet, moving just enough to slip my clothes on and scram out at the first break in combat. When I made my exit, they would still be letting whoops and hollers and whinging the towels, hoping to fray the corners so they'd form skin roses, medals of honor wherever they landed. They'd cheer and yelp with the big hits, laughing at their pustules and carrying on the same way day after day.

I never wanted rose pustules. Risking pain was not in my nature. I was studious and quiet, the kid the movies show with horn-rimmed glasses and enough zits to start a fungus farm. In those junior-high-school years, those years that tested my manhood, I avoided manhood. I never went out behind the shops with the likes of Roger, Larry, and Frank to have a smoke. I never wore my pants around my hips in the style of the day. I didn't even have hips, unlike Jimmy, who got kicked out of Mr. Tolman's class at least once a week for wearing his pants too low. I never went out with busty girls or boasted of conquests at the drive-in movies. I never went out at all. I just studied and practiced the piano and played a little football and basketball with some of the weaker guys on my block.

The biggest risk I ever took in those dark adolescent ages was to hose down Barry the Bully, the biggest, meanest kid in the neighborhood. The magnitude of this accomplishment requires some explanation. Barry was about a month older, five inches taller, and seventy pounds heavier than any kid on the block. When we played games, he made the rules. He decided whether someone was offsides, someone double-dribbled, or someone hit a foul ball. Anyone who objected got his stock line: "Yuh wanna make sumpthin' uv it?"

A well-meaning uncle once bought me some rule books for football and basketball so I could prove to Barry that he was wrong. It was a bad idea. Barry looked at the book, said it was out of date, and claimed that he was right, the book was wrong. It was out of date. The new rules said blah blah blah. I protested, and Barry said, "Yuh wanna make sumpthin' uv it?"

I always wanted to, but I never had the guts. So Barry always won.

Barry won everything—outside of his family, that is. Every night at 5:05, his dad would step onto the porch and whistle a whistle you could hear for blocks. It had the whine of an incoming Scud missile, and my first instinct was to duck and cover. Barry's was to drop whatever he was doing—shooting a basketball or running the football—and scoot for home.

He didn't need to tell the rest of us what would happen if he got home late. We all knew that from his thirteenth birthday party. He had invited Mikey, Gary, Blake, and me—all the boys on the block—to go to the morning cartoons at the Utah Theater on Main Street to celebrate his birthday. This was a big deal: three hours of uninterrupted big-screen cartoons, nonstop Donald Duck, Mickey Mouse, Woody Woodpecker, and Bugs Bunny to a foreground of kids screaming, stomping, and climbing all over each other. I don't remember ever seeing an adult inside the theater on those days. Folks dropped their kids off at nine and hoped they were alive at noon when they came to pick them up.

My mother was to be the driver on the occasion of Barry's thirteenth. Being the gateway into the teens, it was a rite of passage. Mikey, Gary, Blake, and I all sat in the car, groaning that we had to go with Barry—whose parents were paying. Mother pulled up in front of his house, and out came Barry in the very newest, coolest shirt around, a brilliant fluorescent pink one. It was the rage for boys, and I had already begun thinking about one for my birthday, less than a month away.

On Barry's body, there was ever so much more pink and brightness, and he swaggered from the house to the car, grinning broadly, parading his new garb, while we all said wow, that's really cool. I truly loved the shirt, even if it made Barry look like a fluorescent swine. I stepped out of the car to let him in, but before he could get through the door, his little brother began hopping around Barry, pointing at his shirt, cheering, and saying, "See his shirt? See his shirt?"

To make sure we saw it, he grabbed the front of the shirt and pulled it toward our faces. Whereupon every button, literally every button on the shirt popped off and fell to the ground. Everyone sat gaping at the open shirt and Barry's chest. Barry stared downward in disbelief. "I'm not going," he yelled, and ran crying toward the house.

"You are too going," we heard his mother holler from inside. She was a towering woman with a boar's temper.

"No, I'm not."

"Yes, you are."

Barry disappeared into the house. A door inside slammed, and we couldn't hear any more. We sat in the car wondering what to do. My mother said, "We'll just wait a few minutes." The rest of us could hardly suppress our glee at this turn of events. We had suffered too long, heard "Yuh wanna make sumpthin' uv it?" too often to feel any sympathy.

"Tommy," my mother said, after about five long minutes, "why don't you go see if Barry's going?"

I stepped timidly to the open front door. Loud voices emitted from the bedroom.

"Yes, you are."

"No, I'm not."

Sharp, resounding slaps punctuated the dialogue.

25

I had never heard or seen a thrashing before, but this left little to the imagination. "He's getting beaten up," I said when I returned to the car. "I think he's going, though."

Mother waited, and in about five minutes, Barry came out of the house wearing a different shirt, eyes swollen almost shut, face bright red from slapping—about the color of the towel welts from my gym classes. Who knows how his body looked. We drove in silence to the Utah Theater. At the cashier's window, Barry asked for one adult ticket and four children's tickets. I realized that he had planned to show us that he was old enough to buy an adult ticket while the rest of us still needed children's tickets.

Such episodes didn't soften Barry toward the rest of us. One day I was sitting on the front lawn with Blake. We were minding our own business when Barry came up the sidewalk with some instructions for us. Whatever they were, we weren't interested, and we held the high ground. The front lawn of my parents' house consisted of two steep, terraced slopes, dropping about five feet, leveling off for a couple of feet, and then dropping for another five feet. Blake and I were at the top; Barry was giving us orders from below.

To his demands, we probably said something like "drop dead," and he then probably said, "Yuh wanna make sumpthin' uv it?"

Matter of fact, I did. It was time to face the dragon. Just behind me was an outdoor faucet with a hose attached. "Blake," I said, "go to the faucet." I picked up the hose. Barry eyed it and took a couple of steps up the slope. "Come one more step and I'll hose you down," I said. "Blake, when I tell you to turn on the faucet, you turn it on full."

It was High Noon for Barry and me. Barry hesitated, then took a small step toward me to test my resolve. "Don't do it," I repeated.

He took another cautious step.

"Turn it on, Blake," I yelled.

Blake turned the faucet on full. The surge shot straight into Barry's face. I kept the stream focused on his eyes. He was taken aback, tried to flay off the deluge and charge the hill. But I had the nozzle set to hydrant force, and the power of it knocked him backwards. He fell and slid down the grass on his belly, hateful eyes glaring at us, arms splayed out, hands grasping blades of grass to slow his slide. Once at the bottom, he stood and charged the hill again, gasping, groping, snorting. I thought we were going to die. We would die with sweet victory in our hearts, but we would die.

"Run for the back door," I yelled to Blake.

I gave Barry another blast of water, threw down the hose, and ran. Just as Barry reached the crest of the hill, his dad stepped onto the porch and whistled. Barry hesitated. It wasn't hard to imagine what was going through his mind. Should he run us down and beat us raw or go home and explain why he was soaked from top to bottom? Either way, go home on time and wet or go home late and wet, he was going to get a beating. He charged after us. Blake and I got in the back door and locked it just as Barry reached it. We stood in the kitchen, laughing, not believing our good fortune, while Barry pounded furiously on the door, hollering and yelping the cry of someone who was going to be filleted when he went home.

My mother came into the kitchen and asked what on earth was going on.

"Barry was going to beat us up," I said, "and we turned the hose on him and when he was soaked, his dad whistled."

"Well, you little stinks," she said. She was barely stifling a laugh.

She went to the door and, to my horror, opened it. Barry looked like a dripping hairball. "What's the matter, Barry?" she asked.

"Missus Plummer," sob huff gasp, "Tommy and Blake squirted me with the hose and my dad whistled and I'm in trouble." Waah waah waah.

Poor baby.

"Well, you come in and dry out by the oven," Mother said.

I couldn't believe it. She was letting him in. He would beat us up in my own kitchen.

But Mother knew better than that. Barry, in his condition, was not going to beat us up, especially not while she was offering to save his life. So Barry sat in front of the oven door and steamed while Blake and I stood across the room and snickered. Mother gave us dirty looks. Once in a while we'd hear his dad's whistle again, which made Barry wince. It must have taken forty-five minutes for him to dry out enough to go home.

"Thank you, Mrs. Plummer," he said on the way out. He was humility personified.

Barry became a symbol for the great dragon in my life, Fear, the monster that I have to face and defeat again and again. Funny thing about my dragon. It seems to know exactly what I fear and to strike me just there. How does it do that? How can it know what things I'm most chicken about?

In my teenage years, the dragon took the form of sex and girls, pure and simple. Sex, because I knew it was important but I was pretty sure I didn't have it. Girls, because I lusted heavily and never had the cool or sexiness to go after one. My parents asked me one night over dinner if I was going to a church dance the next Saturday. I said I might.

"Well, you better ask someone," my mother said. "Why don't you take Myrtle Monmouth?"

I never could understand why my mother liked Myrtle Monmouth, who had all the radiance of a radish.

"No," I said. "I'll ask Julie Ann."

"Well, do it right now," my mother said.

This was a nasty turn of events. I was plenty self-conscious about asking someone for a date without having my whole family listening in from the kitchen. Younger readers may not remember this, but not so many years ago, we actually had phones connected to a phone cord—and only one phone in the house. You couldn't take it to some secret corner and hide while you were using it. In my case, the phone was in my parents' bedroom. I walked into the bedroom, guts churning, closed the door, got as far away as I possibly could, and dialed. I had this thing with rotary phones when I called girls. I could dial the first six digits, and then I would bring the dial all the way around to where you were supposed to release it, but I couldn't let go. I'd just sit there with my finger in the dial for a while, trying to bolster my courage. Sometimes I'd disconnect and start all over.

Finally, after backing out twice, I released the dial and let the connection go through to Julie. She answered. I was in luck. I hated overly protective and suspicious fathers who answered the phone. It felt like an interview. "Is Julie there?" I'd ask, and he'd say, "May I say who's calling?"—without even saying whether she was there. And then I'd have to say, "Tom Plummer," and realize that my name was full of m's that made it nasally and hard to pronounce, and there'd be a pause while he cycled my name through his little gray cells. Then he'd say, "Just a minute and I'll see," and I could hear a little muffled whispering and then, "She's not here." But this time Julie answered.

"Julie," I said in a low voice to avoid being overheard, "this is Tom Plummer." I probably sounded like a guy with a mouth full of oatmeal.

"Oh," she said. She sounded as if she'd suddenly had a gas attack.

"Will you go to the church dance with me next Saturday night?"

"Yes," she said.

"Good. I'll pick you up at 8:00."

"Okay."

"'Bye."

I walked back into the kitchen. "Wasn't she home?" my mother wanted to know.

"Yes, she was home."

"Well, didn't you talk to her? You were in there all of thirty seconds."

It felt like thirty hours. "Yes, I asked her if she could go, and she said yes."

"Well, didn't you have a little conversation with her?" My mother always worried about my shyness.

"I asked her if she would go to the dance, she said yes, and that's all I needed to know." I couldn't imagine what more there was to say.

My parents looked at each other and laughed. I didn't know what was so funny.

It doesn't take a lot of brains to know that the dragon will be around for the rest of my life and that I'll be just as scared each time it reappears. It'll look a little different—illness and death of family and friends, divorce, widowhood, grief, loneliness, pain, yearning, anger, depression, and guilt.

But slowly I'm realizing that Fear will be here for me to conquer over and over. My first reaction to Fear is to hope someone will take it away—someone like my mother who disarmed Barry with such deft love and competence. Several years ago, Judy Brady wrote an essay called, "Why I Want a Wife." She outlined all the chores that wives traditionally do and concluded that she wanted a wife for herself.

I have a wife. I want a dragon slayer. The funny thing is

that when I call him, the echo always comes back, "He's inside you." It's a sickening thought to know that the Fear Dragon is also inside me, living right next door to my personal St. George. I am St. George; I am the Fear Dragon.

And what about Barry? I don't know. I haven't seen him in years, but I owe him a word of thanks. Barry gave me my first lesson in courage. I owe him one. I also owe him an apology. He led a miserable life. The real dragon, of course, was not Barry. The real dragon was my Fear of Barry. Barry is long gone; the dragon remains. Sometimes it seems so enormous, breathes fire so hot, I can imagine no way of defeating it. Then I turn on the faucet, hose it down, and find that it's not as big as I thought it was.

HELLO, ART MILLER, WHEREVER YOU ARE

Twenty years from now," Mark Twain wrote, "you will be more disappointed by the things you didn't do than by the ones you did do. So throw off the bowlines. Sail away from the safe harbor. Catch the trade winds in your sails. Explore. Dream. Discover." I've had that quote on my computer screen for months at a time, rotating it with others, because it reminds me to live my dreams, to sail away from the safe harbor.

A friend called Louise one day to ask for help along these lines. "Louise," she said, "I don't know how to play. Teach me how to play." This was an intelligent woman, a professional, and she was baffled about play. She had grown up in a strict environment, and play had not been part of family living. Now it was time to learn.

"Okay," Louise said, "we'll go roller skating. We can rent skates at the lake and skate around it on the paths."

"Can you do that?" Lola asked.

"Yes, we can," Louise said. "We can rent the skates at a shop right by the lake. When do you want to go?"

"This afternoon," she said.

Louise told me in an authoritative tone that we were going skating. "Lola needs our help," she said. "She wants to know how to play."

I must have had a baffled look. "Come on," she said. "She wants us to teach her how to play."

Before I knew it, Louise, Lola, Mary (another friend), and I were headed for the lake. We rented skates, sat down at a bench at the edge of the skating lane, and laced them up. I felt shaky. I hadn't been on skates since youth parties when I was thirteen, and I'd lost my touch. Not that I had ever had much of a touch, but I used to be able to skate without looking like I'd just been shot. Now I wobbled out onto the trail, faltered, caught my balance, and did a couple of circles while we waited for Lola to finish up.

Lola hadn't skated before, and this was a brazen and very public act of courage for her. She would learn to play or die. She stood up, wavered, and fell. Not a serious fall, it seemed. She got up again, and we were off. Lola grinned as she survived the first ten yards, let out a whoop or two after the first mile. She was skating. She was learning to have fun.

The trip, we all thought, was a grand success. Late that afternoon Lola called Louise. "I've broken my wrist," she said.

"How did that happen?" Louise was incredulous.

"Remember when I fell just as I stood up?" she said. "I landed on my wrist. I figured it was just sprained, but by the time I got home, it was really hurting. Jerry took me to the emergency room. An X ray showed I had a fracture in my wrist. Come and see my cast."

Lola proudly showed her cast to Louise and me, smiling. "It was worth it," she said.

Adventure has its price. It involves risks. I've reached a point where it's not possible for me to "settle down." At least not yet. I've never liked the idea of settling down—living in the same house, the same neighborhood, the same city for "the rest of my life." My urge is contrary to the model I grew up with. My parents owned the same house for sixty-two years. They took few trips. Their adventures were of other kinds. I've been looking for some contrasting role models.

The first one I remember was a student—Art Miller. Art showed up in my intermediate German course twenty-five years ago looking a lot like Li'1 Abner. He wore big, clunky boots, bib overalls, and an old plaid shirt, and he had a full, bushy beard. I wondered as he walked in if he'd been living in the backwoods of Minnesota. His six-foot-four frame suggested he could be a relative of Paul Bunyan. In my shameful way, I sized him up and passed him off as a hick.

Art was no hick. He got the complex grammar of the first assignment exactly. He participated vigorously in class. He spoke surprisingly good German for a second-year student. I was busy reassessing my first impression of him when he came to my office.

Before he got to his questions, I got to mine. "Tell me about yourself, Art," I said. "Where are you from?"

"I come from a large family in rural Minnesota," he said.

"How large is your family?"

"I'm the youngest of twenty-one."

I took a deep breath. I may have let out a whistle. "You're kidding," I said. "Twenty-one children?"

"Yes."

"Same mother?" This was none of my business, but I just couldn't stifle my curiosity.

"Yes. Same mother, same father."

"Does your father make a lot of money to support that large of a family?" I was now, of course, into stuff that was *really, really* none of my business, but I couldn't stop.

"He's a carpenter," he said. "The kids have made their own way."

Over the next hour of conversation—I held on to Art as long as I could, because I had never met anyone like him—I learned about the life of a survivor. Art told me he had traveled all around the world. He hitched rides on freighters; he shopped for cheap flights and took them wherever they went. Once he had flown to Amsterdam on his way to work on a German farm in Bavaria for the summer. He had planned to hitchhike from Holland. When he went through Dutch customs, the agent, possibly suffering from the same biases I had, asked him how much money he had. Art pulled out three dollars and laid them in front of him.

"Is that all the money you have?" the agent asked.

"Yes."

"You have no other money, no travelers' checks, no credit cards?"

"No other money," Art replied.

Whereupon the agent called security. Art was arrested, charged with vagrancy, and thrown in a holding cell overnight. The next morning Dutch officials sent him back to New York at his own expense.

This did not stop Art. He made many more trips—carefully avoiding the question of how much cash he had with him.

The purpose of his visit to me that day, Art said, was to ask what I knew about hiking through the foothills of the Himalayas.

"I know nothing at all," I said. "I have no idea."

"Well," he said, "I'm trying to talk to as many people as I can. I'm planning to hike through those foothills this summer. I understand it's pretty dangerous for Americans. Villagers don't like us, and a lot of people get killed."

"Are you sure you want to do that?" I asked.

"Oh, I'll be fine," he said.

At the end of the semester, I made a special point of telling Art how glad I was to have met him and to wish him well. He was off to the Himalayas.

I have not heard from him since, but he has been in my head for twenty-five years. Something magical surrounded Art Miller, something powerful. He grew up in poverty, apparently in a kind and decent family, and decided he could do anything he wanted. He was doing anything he wanted. People like that are my heroes. While other students were going to professional school, going to routine jobs, Art Miller was out on an adventure. Has he ever stopped? If he's slowed down a bit, I'm sure he's finding something else to stretch his limits.

I've wondered, as I've read biographies and watched them on television, how it is that so many people who lead stunning lives come out of trying backgrounds. There seems to be something that prods them to get moving. They become writers, journalists, doctors, lawyers, ministers, professors, parents—but even in those lifestyles they stand out because of some personal spin they put on living.

I'm compelled to see life as an adventure because of role models like that. It's a compulsion that says, "You have to live your life while you have it." It's the compulsion that makes Lola get up and skate with a broken wrist. It's the compulsion that makes a cancer patient live the last two months of her life playing, singing, painting, and dancing. It's the compulsion that makes some people put everything on the line to live their life's dream, not because it's a wild dream but because it comes from their very core. It takes great courage to live the adventure that life was meant to be.

For those who are squeamish about such risks, there is a short exercise I found in a magazine years ago and worked through—a prod, if you will, that led me and my young family to Germany for a year. One needs only a pencil and paper and a watch or oven timer. The idea is to do this with time limits of not more than two minutes per exercise—fifteen minutes altogether:

First question: If you knew you were going to die in a month, how would you spend that month? Write down a list of anything that occurs to you as quickly as you can. Two minutes. Don't censor yourself. Just write anything, regardless of how ridiculous.

Second question: If you knew you were going to die in six months, how would you spend that time? Same instructions.

Third question: If you knew you were going to die in a year, how would you spend that time? Same instructions.

Fourth question: If you knew you were going to die in five years, how would you spend that time?

Now take two minutes and go over the four lists. Strike out anything that is so off the wall that it's not worth even considering—like, "I want to live on the dark side of the moon."

From each of the four lists choose the three things you want most.

Now, from those twelve items, list the three you want most. Write down one thing you can do today toward your first choice. Write down three things you can do this week toward all three. Put them on your bathroom mirror where you'll see them every day.

Adventure may bring hardship. I was impressed by a news article I read about Dr. Jerri Nielsen, a physician who treated her own breast cancer for several months while stationed in Antarctica. She cared for herself until the weather warmed enough for a plane to land and return her to the United States. Cancer, she said, made her appreciate life even more than living in the most frigid place on earth. "When you get cancer," she said, "the same thing happens. You don't have to go away to find the frontier."

I've latched on to these stories. They tell me that comfort is not necessarily the way to go; that security is not necessarily happiness; that stretching myself to the limits—shrinking as they are—brings growth; that living adventures of whatever kind is one way to multiply the talents God gave me. Whether leaving or staying, straying or settling down, my heroes are those who grab hold—who, at whatever cost, put their lives at risk to live more fully. It's an optimism I can live with. I don't know if adventurers live longer, but they certainly know they're alive.

A FEW DUCKS
AND A SANDPILE

When our oldest son, Jonathan, turned three, we decided to send him to nursery school. Nursery school, we knew, was a place where children learned social skills and got a good foundation for entering school. It was also a time to give us a little break.

So on a day in early September, after being notified that "we" had been accepted to the program, we went to the University of Minnesota nursery school to meet with Steve, Jonathan's new teacher. Steve wore his long, curly hair in a ponytail, had a full beard, and spoke with a Brooklyn accent. His plaid shirt, jeans, and running shoes suggested this was a man who was comfortable with himself. He had a doctorate in child development from the University of Michigan, spoke with confidence and warmth about the Minnesota program and his relationship with children, and took us through the phases of a daily routine.

"First," he said, "children get their throats checked by the nurse. If the throat is red, they go home. Then comes free time, meaning that the children have the option to engage in any play they want." The room was filled with good stuff for kids—a sandbox, building blocks, hiding places, a puppet theater, books—everything that might appeal to young imaginations. "After free time comes more structured play—acting, reading, singing—and then less structure."

It was a routine designed to put the children at ease and let them get accustomed to a friendly learning environment. Parents were free to watch at any time from an observation booth perched over the classroom.

"And, Jonathan," Steve said, "my name is Steve. Call me Steve."

As the year passed, Jonathan showed signs of growth and comfortable development.

That summer we left for Berlin, where I had research planned for the next several months. When we settled in, we decided to continue the nursery school experience. Now, I reasoned, Jonathan would also learn German. I would be able to speak German with one of my sons.

"Kids pick up a language without even knowing it," I told Louise in my most pedantic voice.

She reminded me that she knew this, since she had been born in Holland and learned English in an American school.

I did some research and found a tidy little nursery school not far from our apartment. We paid a visit.

The teacher, Frau Grimmelshausen, was an uptight young woman who showed not one bit of Steve's comfortable attitude. Although school was held five mornings a week from eight to noon, she informed us that Jonathan should begin with three mornings a week, from eight to ten.

"This will give him a chance to get used to us and us to him," she said. "Then he can come full time."

I felt uneasy. How would Jonathan adjust to this new and obviously more structured environment, when she was cutting him out of a large portion of it?

"And," she said, "each child brings a piece of fruit to eat every day."

I set my discomfort aside by assuring myself that Jonathan would become acquainted with another culture.

On the first day, Louise dropped an apple in a brown lunch sack, and I packed Jonathan off to school. Frau Grimmelshausen greeted each child at the door. Each shook her hand and said, "Guten Morgen, Frau Lehrerin." (Good morning, Mrs. Teacher.) The girls made a little curtsy, the boys a bow as they said this. That was the German way.

Remembering Steve's relaxed atmosphere and Jonathan's tendency to erupt, I struggled to keep a calm demeanor. When his turn came, Frau Grimmelshausen tutored him through the routine several times. I could see his entire nervous system recoiling as she shook his hand, bent him at the waist in a stiff bow, and rehearsed, "Guten Morgen, Frau Lehrerin."

Jonathan tried hard to respond in the German he couldn't understand, to a culture he could not comprehend. She made him try again. And again. By now he was twitching. I was twitching. Finally she directed him to a waiting room—I think of it now as a holding pen—where all the children sat stiffly around a table, without speaking or whispering, with their fruit placed in front of them. To my embarrassment, each child had a carefully sculpted piece of fruit that his or her mother or father must have taken an hour to carve into some neat shape—a duck, a kitty, or a star. I imagined mothers getting up at five in the morning to begin sculpting the fruit, casting off failed attempts for fruit salad. Jonathan put his apple in front of him and sat down, his leg convulsing like a trout yanked out of water.

According to instructions, I came at ten to pick him up. The school was in full swing, but Jonathan had to leave. Frau Grimmelshausen told me the first day had gone pretty well. She said she had set him up in front of the group, introduced the new little classmate from America, and had the students shout in chorus, "Good morning, Jonathan," in English. "I wanted him to feel right at home," she said. Then she stayed with him as he played with the other children, breaking in to translate conversations. I imagined Jonathan thinking of places to hide from her as she chased him frantically around the room. To my suggestion that she might just let him play with the other children and pick up the language on his own, she said no. Then he wouldn't understand what was going on.

At home that night, Jonathan was wild. Tantrums. Fits. After a one-day break, school came again. Louise carved up an apple as best she could, cursing under her breath, slicing her finger.

After three days of school, we withdrew him. The

tantrums subsided, and Louise settled into her own routine with Jonathan and his younger brother, Edmund, at the local park, where they took a bag of toys, played in the sand, and fed the ducks at the pond.

Jonathan says he remembers none of the nursery school experience. He does remember the ducks.

The question I keep asking myself is this: What are my ducks? What is my sandpile?

In the last few years, I have discovered the ocean. It's not that I've never seen it before, but I've begun to see the ocean in a more spiritual light, as the pulse of the earth, a reflection of my own pulse. I noticed it one year when we rented a small beach house with our friends Al and Ginny. We arrived at three or four in the morning, after driving most of the night. I stepped into our little bedroom, opened the window, and heard, for the first time in several years, the roar of the surf down below the house. It was a magical, powerful sound— the sound of creation. I stood spellbound for several minutes, just listening.

For the next several days, we walked every day down the long flight of stairs to spend several hours on the beach. Sometimes we just sat. Other times we walked. Al had brought a fishing pole and line for ocean casting. He caught a small shark, which we baked and ate that night, and a guitar fish, one of the ugliest creatures in the sea, which he gave to some immigrants who watched him reel it in. They were deliriously happy to accept it, jumping around like frogs and passing it through the group. Al later learned that the guitar fish has a wonderful flavor, that he had given away the better fish of his catch.

To go to the ocean is to go to the source of life. Magical things are concealed in the deep—fish of all kinds, monsters, mermaids. It is a place of danger, of foreboding, a destructive power that captures our imagination whenever we hear of the sinking of the *Titanic* and of ships carrying gold bullion. We love to flirt with its power and to escape with our lives.

I'm a sinker, not a swimmer, but I can't resist getting in a kayak when the water is bathtub calm, paddling out a ways, and sitting quietly while the water gently rocks me. The anxieties of everyday life, the pressure for competence, for excellence, for performance seems no larger than a piece of seaweed against that vast surface. My mind lightens, and I try to scan the cadences of the rocking water, cadences far more eloquent, more varied, more harmonious than cadences the finest poets can write. Here is a place of peace, a place of rhythm, a place as ancient as creation itself, a place as close to God now as it was when he said, "Let the waters bring forth abundantly the moving creature that hath life, and fowl that may fly above the earth in the open firmament of heaven. . . . And God saw that it was good" (Genesis 1:20–21). I sit on the water and feel the pulse of God. And it is good.

A LITTLE CREATIVITY, A LOT OF TOLERANCE

Al has started making his own bricks. This has been years in coming. When Louise and I used to drop by for a chat with Al and Ginny, we noticed that some of the bricks in the walk to their house had begun to weather and crumble. This, of course, was making the walk a little dangerous, especially on winter days. But it was really not so much a matter of safety as a foreshadowing of work to be done. Once in a while Al would grumble a bit about the walk, but other than that not much was said or done. After all, other people have cracks in their sidewalks and spots where trees have pushed the concrete out of shape. But I believe that way back in the recesses of Al's mind was a little gnome on the lookout for a solution.

The solution germinated the day when Al and Ginny, Louise, and I visited the Johannes Hundertwasser apartment buildings in Vienna. It is an attraction to sightseers because Hundertwasser has done something outrageously unconventional in staid and proper old Vienna. He challenged both the theory of modernist architecture, which calls for straight, uncluttered lines, open spaces, and sparse décor and the tradition of nineteenth-century Viennese architecture, which calls for baroque, rococo, and Renaissance buildings with a touch of ancient Rome thrown in. Hundertwasser has written how modern architecture, with its unnatural geometric shapes, drains the life out its structures. Trees and flowers and shrubs aren't straight, he said. They have an organic feeling. Nothing in nature is absolutely straight. So, he reasoned, the modern architects were really opposing life and nature.

Hundertwasser followed nature. Almost nothing, including walls, ceilings, and floors, is straight in a Hundertwasser building. Pillars rise at oblique angles. Rooms have floors so wavy, you have to watch your every step. Bricks in primary colors are splashed randomly into walls. Trees grow out of arboretums sprinkled up the outsides of buildings, and, as a spoof, a piece of a traditional Viennese apartment building from the nineteenth century has been left in place and enveloped in the new structure. To add personal variety, apartment owners may decorate around the outsides of their own windows as far as they can reach. Some have painted figures around the frames, some colors. A roundish fountain outside the main entrance features a tiled figure of a serpent that coils around the complete circumference, with its large head emerging from the water on one side.

A restaurant in the Kunst-Haus Museum a few blocks away, which holds much of Hundertwasser's artwork, has wavy, uneven, black-and-white tile floors and a living ceiling of blooming, potted flowers intertwined into crosswires. The rest rooms evoke all the queasiness of an amusement park fun house.

Everywhere around the apartment buildings and museum, people are smiling, because here is a project against the tyranny of convention, and it has won an amazing victory. I would not want all of the buildings in the world to look like the Hundertwasser Haus. Then we would be living in sameness again. But it's an inspiring thing to see a single creative effort that makes everyone happy, Viennese and tourists alike.

Al walked around Hundertwasser's Mad Hatter creations smiling, making little comments. Something was cooking in his head, but he didn't give anything away. He and Ginny returned home in June. By the time we visited them in August, we saw that Al had made changes in his brick walk. New, decorative bricks replaced old, crumbling ones, bricks with colorful pieces of broken glass, fake jewelry, doll cups and saucers, anything he cared to implant. They lit up his walk like a path into Alice's world. It wasn't a one-time thing for Al. His bricks could be removed so that on special occasions—Halloween, Christmas, Easter, birthdays—special bricks appeared: bricks with pumpkins, masks, and goblins; blinking Christmas tree lights; Easter bunnies and plastic eggs; "welcome home" bricks for children who've been away.

This is the scientist-doctor-artist-of-the-walkway, whose high-school counselor reviewed his aptitude tests and told him he should become a cheese wrapper. *Que será, será.*

Closet artists are everywhere. Take my sister-in-law Marilyn. Marilyn is a fanatic garage-sale shopper. On

WALTZING TO A DIFFERENT STRUMMER

Saturday mornings, when most people are sleeping in, Marilyn gets up at six and by seven is on the doorsteps of people who have advertised garage sales. She gets the pick of the litter. She has collected an amazing array of stuff for pennies over the years, but it's not just her uncanny ability to get good deals that merits kudos—it's her eye for recirculating things that ordinary folks like me pass up as junk. In her house, decorated in country style, is an old wooden screen door on the china cabinet in the dining room. On her dining-room table is a wooden tray for French bread that she has filled with buttons from her mother's sewing kit. Around the living room is an array of unlikely accessories:

an antique pitchfork leaning against the wall, tines up

two old suitcases next to an overstuffed chair

an old milk pail filled with worn croquet mallets and pegs on the hearth

an antique coat rack with hooks on a frame hanging above the fireplace mantle

a water pump on a table in the corner

an ancient fan on the piano

a sign over the bay window: Victoria Station

a rusty mailbox hanging on the wall

a school desk and chairs

an abacus, a game of jacks, a wire basket, and a bouquet of flowers on a worn table

The amazing thing is that all this "junk" works together, creating new harmonies. Marilyn looks at farm implements, fishing gear, and old board games and sees décor. To walk into

A LITTLE CREATIVITY, A LOT OF TOLERANCE

Marilyn's living room is as inspiring as to make a trip to the Hundertwasser Haus. She has broken the rules of convention and in the process created a living, breathing space.

I think of creativity as seeing and doing things differently from everyone else. Truly creative types swim against the swift current of convention. This sometimes gets them into troubled waters, because some folks don't like the boat being rocked.

They complain, as I did years ago when Louise started moving the Uiterhovens' furniture around. Louise and I, through a chain of acquaintances, were asked to housesit for the Uiterhovens one summer. We were all too happy to abandon our stuffy little apartment in Cambridge for the shady environs of an upscale neighborhood. The home was, to my recollection, tasteful, clean, not sumptuous, but sensibly decorated. That was good enough for me. Not for Louise. On our first morning there, she began shoving sofas, chairs, and tables around. I asked her what she was doing.

"I'm rearranging the furniture," she said. "Can't you see their arrangement doesn't work?"

"No," I said.

"Come on," she said, "help me move this sofa."

After just four years of marriage, I knew enough not to fight the flow. We moved the furniture around, and voilà. The Uiterhovens' living room was transformed into Louise's living room. I've come to recognize this as a confluence of energies in Louise. First is a powerful nesting instinct, which demands that her living conditions be her own. It doesn't matter if the

Shah's designer himself has decorated the room, Louise will change it into her own. Second is a powerful creative instinct that sees spaces and objects in configurations that I cannot see, and which demands that things be put right. I've learned just to go along with this.

Psychologist Dr. Phil was on *Oprah* recently listening to a man complaining about his wife. She was a compulsive furniture mover, he said, and he described a day that he had spent moving furniture around his living room into different configurations. First this way, then that way, then back to the original plan. I suppose this had worn him out, and he was now asking the psychologist how he could cure his wife. "Do you have a suggestion for me?" he asked.

"Yep, I do," Dr. Phil said without taking a breath. "Just go with the flow, Mike."

Creative people have a hard time staying out of trouble because they are always frightening the more staid members of society. In Great Britain, for example, another club is upset. An article in *The Times* the other day bore the title, "Toy dog raises its mating game." It announced that a Chihuahua has been crossed with a Labrador in an attempt to develop the perfect dog for people who are hearing impaired.

It seems some folks in a charity for the deaf in Great Britain were trying to figure out how to create better "hearing ear" dogs, which let their owners know when someone is at the door, when the alarm goes off, or when a Scud missile is on its way. They wanted an animal that was gentle but not so large as a Labrador, one that had hearing acute enough to pick up a horse's whinny in the royal stables half a field away.

Someone in the office owned a Chihuahua and someone else owned a Labrador. During a think-tank session, they got the idea of cross-pollinating them. If nothing else, they finally found a use for the Chihuahua.

There was, however, the problem of size in breeding the dogs, which creative minds also solved. The result has been a litter of six "Labrahuahua" puppies, which will soon undergo training for their future masters. Unfortunately, the article did not have an accompanying photograph, so my mind continues ceaselessly to create images of just what these creatures look like. Still, I look forward to the day when they are adopted into the American Kennel Club as a new breed, and every pet store carries a new book on the darling "Labrahuahua," whose ears serve worthy purposes.

This will be over the dead bodies of proud British Chihuahua owners. The article reports that Diana Fitt-Savage, of Sandringham, Norfolk, secretary of the British Chihuahua Club, said: "It's just unnatural. One vet who heard about it told me 'It's a wonder they didn't lose the Chihuahua.'"

I must wonder at Ms. Fitt-Savage's comment about the whole thing being unnatural. The entire history of dogs is fraught with unnatural breeding. How did a Chihuahua come about in the first place, if someone wasn't fooling around with some "unnatural" ideas? I know enough about such things from working in the family garden to be quite certain that this most unnatural of all dogs did not happen on the first try. My mother spent summers cross-pollinating iris, creating ever-more spectacular and curious combinations with each new generation.

Our dog Zoe is a case in point. Zoe is a bichon frisé, a breed created especially as a lap dog for French royalty. She's a little, white, fluffy dog, the kind Gary Larson likes to see squashed in his cartoons, the kind I swore I'd never own after growing up with setters, except that Louise fell for Zoe one afternoon on an ill-fated adventure to a pet store. "Oh, she's darling," she said. "And look how she snuggles in to me." It was true. Zoe was nestling her little white body against Louise's chest, licking her chin, wagging her little fluffy tail, saying, as best a dog could, "I'm yours. Take me."

We did not take Zoe that day. I convinced Louise that we must do the sensible thing. A dog is a huge investment in time and energy, not to mention carpet cleaner, I reminded her. And we must do what we have agreed to do (having previously made disastrous spontaneous purchases). We must give this decision twenty-four hours. The next afternoon, just twenty-four hours later, we were back in the pet store buying Zoe. And Zoe has been absolutely true to her unnatural breeding. She won't get off you. Not ever. If you are sitting down, she's in your lap. If you are lying in bed, she nestles into your back. If you are in the car, she has to sit on your lap in the front seat. My compliments to the breeders.

It seems to me that underneath all of this fervor about clubs and breeds and ethnic-dog-breed purity is something dangerous about human beings and being human. It smacks of prejudice. It doesn't take much to turn an insider into an outsider—just a little something "unnatural," maybe just the wrong shoes, and poof, you're out. Getting back in may be harder than knocking down the walls of Jericho.

When I was on Prince Edward Island a few years ago, I learned that people not born on the island are referred to as being "from away." During that trip I heard a news commentary about a man who died at age ninety-eight. The report said he was "from away." He was born on the Magdalen Islands, just a ferry ride away, and immigrated with his parents to Prince Edward Island when he was two. He had spent ninety-six of his ninety-eight years on the island, but he was still "from away."

Several studies were undertaken at Stanford University after World War II, in the wake of the Holocaust experience, to determine the thinking of people who were capable of ordering the extermination of entire ethnic groups. One of the unsettling findings, published in a book called *The Authoritarian Personality,* was that the Nazi mentality was not limited to Germans. It extended to the entire human race, including Americans, who have made their own remarkable contributions to racism and sexism.

At the other extreme, I know a Caucasian artist who needed a heart transplant. When he received a donor heart that saved his life, he wanted to know who the donor had been. He was told by whatever powers that this was not possible. The identity of heart donors is not available to the recipients. But he wanted to thank this donor in his own way, so he managed to pull some strings and learned, finally, that the donor who had saved his life was an African-American woman. He is very grateful. All of his paintings now have beside his name a heart with the initials of his donor.

Of course, creativity has its limits. A report came to my e-mail once about a creative solution to removing a beached whale that had died. The facts, as I recall them, were that the whale had landed on a popular beach in Oregon, and, as is the way with dead beached whales, it had begun to stink. The townspeople, fearing the demise of their tourist trade, conspired to get rid of it. Some guys with enlarged egos got their recreational boats together, tied ropes around the whale, and tried to tow it off the beach. They couldn't move it. Then a local tugboat tried to pull it away. Nothing. The whale lay there and stank and stank and stank.

Desperate, the town had a brainstorming session. What could they do to save themselves and their summer tourist trade? Someone suggested they could dynamite the whale off the beach. This seemed like a very good idea. I suspect it appealed most to the guys who used to put firecrackers under tin cans to see how high they could blow them. And maybe there was someone in the group like me, who discovered that if you put enough explosives under the can, like a cherry bomb, the can just disappears. There's a loud boom, and it's gone.

That kind of mentality must have prevailed in the meeting in Oregon. A local explosives team was assembled, and they loaded a whole lot of dynamite into the whale, I assume wearing perfumed masks. Folks gathered from miles around to say good-bye.

A LITTLE CREATIVITY, A LOT OF TOLERANCE

There was a countdown, tensions rose, guys probably expected to see the best display ever of their firecracker experiments. At liftoff, there was a mighty boom, and the whale, like my tin cans, just disappeared. It was literally gone. Not a smidgen remained on the beach. Where it went, no one knew. What mattered was that it was gone. The crowd let out a mighty roar—cheering, hollering, dancing—and then, in the middle of the festivities, great chunks of whale began to fall out of the sky. Five-hundred-pound clumps of lard landing on Land Rovers and Miatas. The rain falleth on the just and the unjust. People were screaming for help, running for their lives as the great whale took its revenge on the maniacal crowd. It was a bad moment in the history of creativity. The report I read didn't say how long it rained whale or what happened to tourism that year.

Creativity had run amok. But creative folks will try something like it again, because creativity is a state of mind that searches for new ways of doing things, seeing things, and being in the world, and it stops for no one. It isn't that everything is as great or memorable as the Mona Lisa. It's just that in a creative mindset one refuses to accept conventionality and tradition. It may be as simple as getting out of a long line of cars by turning right and making a U-turn rather than waiting to turn left. It may be as small as having something witty and wonderful to say to someone who is sick. It may be as easy as saying $E=MC^2$. Creative minds make the world a little better, a little less predictable, and a whole lot saner. I'm reminded of that every time I walk up to Al's door.

A LITTLE
SOMETHING TO LOVE

There comes a point in life when people get something they want because they've wanted it for a long, long time. They've exercised restraint, been frugal and long-suffering, maybe even gloated when they heard the neighbors were going to debt counseling. They've bought their children's clothes at factory-second stores and told them to punch anyone who points out the "IRREGULAR" stamped on the back pocket of their jeans. They've stayed at home rather than taking a dream trip that they've got earmarked in a ten-year-old *National Geographic,* which they keep under the bed and read secretly at night when their spouse is asleep. But at a certain point, maybe after an illness, maybe just after years of self-discipline, they snap. They see this dream thing, whatever it is, and they say, "I don't care. I'm going to have it. I'm ready for the consequences. I'm not going to die without having it just once." And they lay out the cash, lie awake many nights in secret repentance, but rejoice in their hearts that they've realized a lifelong dream.

A LITTLE SOMETHING TO LOVE

In 1949 my parents decided to replace their 1936 Ford. It had been breaking down all too often. This came to a head the night my parents took a guest from out of town to a restaurant some distance away. His son and I went along. After a lovely dinner, as Dad was nursing the old Ford over a mountain pass, it overheated. Vapor lock, they used to call it. So he got out, lifted the hood, and tried to see in. It was late, and the moon provided the only light. Squinting even to see the radiator cap, Dad ducked his head farther and farther under the hood, feeling for loose wires. At that moment, a car came around the bend from the opposite direction. The visitor's son, a kid about sixteen and full of himself, leaned forward from the backseat and honked the horn to warn the oncoming car that we were there. Dad's head was now inches from the horn. He reared up, bashed his head on the hood latch, and, as my grandmother used to say, took the Lord's name in vain. He demanded to know who had hit the horn, and the boy confessed. "Don't touch that %#$$^% horn again," Dad yelled.

Such moments under the hood added pressure to the idea of shopping for a new car. So Mom and Dad began visiting car dealerships. I went along, thrilled at the prospects. They test-drove Packards, Studebakers, Hudsons, Buicks, and, yes, Fords. I loved the luxurious feel of the Hudsons and Packards, with their lush interiors and seats so sumptuous that the old Ford began feeling like a Radio Flyer. It was obvious to me that my mother loved the larger, more cushy cars and despised the smaller ones, particularly the Fords. At her

59

insistence, we returned several times to the Buick dealership to see a 1949 Buick with Dynaflow—the new automatic transmission. It was pale blue with a long, sloping back that made it seem quite pre–space age, and a hood that extended at least three or four times as far out as the Ford's. "Important Person Coming Through," it seemed to say. This was a real car. It shifted gears without so much as a tiny jolt, not at all like the stick shift in the old Ford. I watched Mother as she lovingly touched the Buick and stiffened up when she got near the Fords.

My dad's attraction to cars was quite different: cheap, essential, and simple. The old Ford had been pretty reliable—up to the last few years—hadn't it? It wasn't all that much trouble to add water to the radiator every 100 miles, was it? Did Utah really have so many mountains? Did we really need the Buick's posh interior and the gas-guzzling Dynaflow? Did we really need to shell out the extra $1,000 for the Buick? Even I could tell that he wasn't listening to the hints Mother was sending him. She never said, "Gail, I want the Buick. Buy me the Buick." That kind of directness was not her style.

The moment of decision is all too clear in my memory. We were standing in the Ford dealership next to the car my mother, I knew, really didn't want. It was a dark red 1949 Ford with four door handles that you pulled like levers, and stick shift with overdrive—Dad loved the overdrive—for fuel economy on trips. Mom stood quietly, patiently by, watching, hating every moment. Her pursed lips and tightly folded arms said all that needed to be said.

Dad turned to her and said, "What do you think?"

"It's up to you," she said.

"Okay," he said to the salesman, "we'll take this one." He arranged for delivery the next day.

As we drove home in the '36 Ford, Mother was crying. Now that I've been married as long as my parents were in their entire lives, I think I get it.

"Did you want that Buick?" Dad asked.

"You know I wanted that Buick," she said. "I loved it. And you went right ahead and bought another darned old Ford."

"Then I'll cancel the Ford and buy the Buick," Dad said.

"No," she said. "It's too late now. We'll have the Ford."

Why didn't Mom speak up? Why didn't she say she wanted the Buick? She had an opening in the Ford dealership when Dad asked what she thought. All she had to say was, "If you buy that Ford, I'll murder you in your sleep."

For ten years she waited quietly for another chance. Then one day, at the same Buick dealership, she spotted a gorgeous Buick Special, a hardtop convertible with a tomato-red top, white body, chrome bumpers the size of caskets, and side trim to die for. It stood proudly in the window and said, "Buy me, Elva, I'm yours."

"Isn't it beautiful," Mom said. It was not a question.

My dad, having healed from the wounds of 1949, arranged for a test-drive. It was truly gorgeous. Enormous tires with white sidewalls, hubcaps the size of spaceships. I put more than my share of words into supporting Mom because I now had a driver's license, and that was going to be a cool car for dates.

That night Dad called the salesman. "We'll buy the car. But I won't pay more than $2,400 for it."

"Sorry, Mr. Plummer," the salesman said. "The price is $2,600, not a penny less." This car had all the comforts of home, he said. It had every feature imaginable. It had been specially ordered by the owner's wife and driven by her for just a short time. It had the trappings of an imperial carriage. Twenty-six hundred was the price. Firm.

"Call me back if you change your mind," Dad said.

To this day, I can feel a surge of rage and frustration shoot up my spine. My dad could be so stinking stubborn, he would put his marriage on the line for a lousy $200. "What are you going to do if he doesn't come down?" I asked.

"Not buy it," he said.

A few minutes later the phone rang. It was the salesman. "Mr. Browning says he can't sell the car for less than $2,500," he said.

"That won't do," my dad said. "Not a dollar more than $2,400."

I have felt less pain from a proctologist. Mother sat quietly in the living room. Why wasn't she speaking up? Time passed. A long time. The phone rang. The salesman told Dad he could have the car for $2,400.

It was a jubilant moment for the family. The 1949 Ford, which my dad had sold to my sister and her husband, was long forgotten. Long dead, actually—it had disappeared around 1954. Dad had replaced it with a used Buick he bought from a neighbor. Now he was fully forgiven. *Redeemed* may be more accurate.

The next morning we picked up the Buick. Mother drove it home. Being a tiny woman, she sat on a pillow so she could see the road ahead. She was a proud owner of the most beautiful car in town, a five-foot woman with 350 horses at her command, an automatic transmission, and enough chrome for a queen.

It remained her car until 1994, thirty-six years later, when she could no longer see well enough to drive. She sold it for $2,500 to a man who restores cars and who had a hard time believing that this gorgeous dinosaur had 63,000 original miles. Truly a car driven by a little old lady. He started it up in the garage, but it wouldn't budge. It had sat there so long that the brakes were frozen. He had to drag it out of the garage like an angry child that doesn't want to leave home.

Before he took it away, Mother wanted her picture taken standing by the car. I took pictures from several angles, long view, corner view, and side view. The side view shows it best, a tiny lady, ninety-two years old, standing alongside eighteen feet of antiquity, the one thing she asked for herself. She smiles brightly into the camera, but the smile masks the tears she shed when they towed the old car away. "I want a copy of the pictures," she said as the car disappeared around the corner.

ANONYMITY HAS ITS LIMITS

Anonymity did not run in my family. My father was a speech teacher and spoke all over our state and in many others. His motto was, "Ya gotta get 'em laughing." It's not possible to stay anonymous and keep people laughing. When he came home after giving a speech, I would sometimes ask him how it went. "Oh," he'd say, "they were a bit slow at first, but I got 'em moving pretty well." He always hit his audience head on: "I'm glad to be here and look into your faces. Heaven knows there are faces here that ought to be looked into." I recently came across several pages of his openers.

Of the volumes of poetry he memorized and recited, he loved Robert Burns's the most, possibly because Robert Burns had an in-your-face attitude, possibly because Dad could practice a Scottish accent:

> O ye, wha are sae guid yoursel,
> Sae pious and sae holy,
> Ye've nought to do but mark and tell

ANONYMITY HAS ITS LIMITS

Your neebours' fauts and folly;
Whase life is like a weel-gaun mill,
Supplied wi' stor o' water;
The heapet happer's ebbing still,
An' still the clap plays clatter!

Dad recited Burns annually at President David O. McKay's birthday parties and for meetings of the Salt Lake Scottish Society. He was particularly proud of these performances since he had not a single drop of Scottish blood in his veins. Recently I popped into the Scottish store in downtown Salt Lake. The clerk asked my name, which he repeated several times after I told him. "Plummer. Plummer. You related to Gail Plummer?"

"I'm his son," I said.

"He used to recite Robert Burns for our meetings. He was terrific. I haven't heard from him for a while."

"He died in 1964," I said.

When Mom and Dad picked me up in Vienna at the end of my mission, we began a tour of Europe in Austrian cities where I had worked. "We'll go to the Linz branch on Sunday," I said. "They'll want us all to speak. I can translate for you."

"I'm going to give my talk in German," Dad said. "I had a year in high school." On Saturday night, he sat down and began writing the talk. When he'd done as much as he could, he handed it to me. "Here, you fix it up. I'm going to wind it up with a poem I learned." I straightened the grammar, filled in the gaps, and he set about rehearsing his talk, just as he rehearsed every talk he ever gave.

Sunday came, and we were invited to speak. I had served thirteen months in the Linz branch. These were my friends. Mom went first; I translated. Then Dad. He stood in front of the congregation with all the confidence of a ringmaster. He belted out his talk loud and clear, his accent better than most, and finished with his poem, which he introduced by saying, "And now, brothers and sisters, this is how I feel about you":

> Ich bin Dein
> Du bist Mein,
> Des sollst Du gewiss sein.
> Du bist verschlossen
> In meinem Herzen,
> Drinnen musst Du immer sein.

> *I am yours,*
> *You are mine.*
> *Of that you can be sure.*
> *You are locked in my heart*
> *There you must always stay.*

He closed and sat down beaming. Dad loved a good show. When the meeting ended, the members mobbed him, speaking thanks and praise in German, patting him on the shoulders, shaking his hand. He said "Dankeschön," again and again, because he had used up all of his German and then some and had no idea what they were saying to him.

"You get us through Austria, Switzerland, and Germany," he said as we drove away. "I'll get us through France. I had two years in college."

In Paris, he walked up to the concierge of the Hotel California (its real name) and said, "Parlez-vous Français?"

The concierge looked at him long and hard and said, "Oui."

"We want a room for three," Dad said in his clearest English.

I have photocopied two volumes of public-speaking material that Dad used, everything from homilies to jokes to poetry to speeches he gave at high-school graduations and funerals. He gave dozens of talks in support of funding a new library and planetarium for Salt Lake City, and those are preserved as well. If there's a single impression that I get from all of that material, it is that my father knew his causes and went after them. If there were any imperatives in what he did to accomplish his ends, they were (1) to have a sense of humor, and (2) to speak out about his convictions. Anonymity was never part of his thinking.

In 1956 the mayor of Salt Lake City invited Dad to be the keynote speaker at a celebration for the fiftieth anniversary of the Salt Lake Library. The library was in a beautiful old building on State Street, but it had become woefully inadequate as a library for the city—had been declared inadequate, as a matter of fact, in 1914 by an eminent visiting librarian. Dad told the gathering of dignitaries that this celebration was a sham, that they were memorializing a building that had long since served its purpose, that they had a horse-and-buggy library. "It seems like such a strange thing to *celebrate,*" he said, "something like my celebrating your twentieth anniversary in a prison or mental institution." Soon thereafter, Dad became chair of the library board, and after much political toil and trouble, the new library was finally dedicated on October 30, 1964, one week after he died.

With this upbringing, silence has come hard for me. I have learned, however, that anonymity has its place. I learned it at Fort Ord in 1958. A drill sergeant was hollering at the company through a dense fog that we were supposed to brush our teeth before breakfast, not after breakfast. It was 5:30 in the morning, and we could not see him, only hear him bark, and for this we had to get up and put on fatigues, combat boots, and a cap that looked like a pea-soup can. "Whoever heard of brushing your teeth after breakfast?" he yelled. "Does anyone here—anyone at all—have parents so stupid that they told you to brush your teeth *after* breakfast?"

Was any one of us so dedicated to the truth that he would have yelled back, "Sergeant, with all due respect, my father and mother, both members of Mensa International, always taught me to brush my teeth after breakfast. Otherwise, I'd carry food from breakfast in my teeth until after dinner, thereby accelerating tooth decay." No one spoke up. To speak up was to ask to do ten push-ups on the fog-moistened asphalt in front of the rest of the company.

One guy did speak up on another topic once. The sergeant had him down on the ground "giving him ten" before he knew what had happened. In his defiance the soldier, an athlete, did them on one hand, whereupon the sergeant made him do ten more on the other hand.

We all knew what the guy with the power wanted: absolute, unquestioning obedience, cleanliness in its purest form. Anonymity. Sameness. We made beds, polished floors, scoured sinks and toilets in the barracks before breakfast. If we went to the lavatory or brushed our teeth after breakfast, as someone had obviously done that morning, we were going to get more misery than we ever dreamed possible. The strategy in the military was to punish everyone for one man's transgression. That way the transgressor got punished, and everyone else made sure he didn't do it again.

It was a variation on a rule I learned on the first day in boot camp. Be invisible. Don't look into anyone's eyes; don't mess anything up. Don't argue with someone of higher rank. Keep your hat bill pulled down over your eyes and disappear.

Anonymity had its virtues in combat training as well. Keep your head down. That was the rule. Stick your head up, become a person, and a sniper is going to blow you away. The key to survival was keeping your head down. Just like "duck and cover," which we learned when I was in grade school training to survive nuclear attack. If you look at the brilliant flash of light, our teachers would say, it will blind you and you'll die. They never told us the survival statistics or showed us photos of survivors in Nagasaki and Hiroshima. So, in the army, we would practice keeping our heads down, running from tree to tree, hill to hill, hole to hole, keeping our heads down.

I wondered during rifle training, hand-to-hand-combat, and grenade throwing just how I could keep my head down if I also had to kill the enemy. I supposed I could stand up, bend over, and keep my head down while shooting an automatic rifle, but then I would be looking backwards through my legs. That wasn't worth pointing out to the officers; in combat training, your job is not to think but to do what you're told. So I never asked, and I never had to do pushups for thinking. Stand out, and you've got a problem.

My problem with being invisible was that the dirtiest, foulest, most conspicuous guy in the company had the name Roland Plummer. There were only two Plummers in the company, and I was symbolically and symbiotically attached to the Pig. Everyone pretty much ignored R.P. Then came the time for our first leave off base, the first time out of Fort Fogbound in four weeks. After four weeks on base, everyone in the company was suffering from cabin fever bordering on hallucinations.

But the army has its ways. Before letting us have the weekend off, First Lieutenant Baer, the company commander, had to inspect us, wearing his white gloves. He had to look at the neatness of our lockers and the tightness of our beds. He had to run his clean gloves along the tops of doors and behind the toilets, and they'd better not come back soiled. We scrubbed, waxed, and dusted. We scraped shower walls and polished toilet seats. We were ready.

Baer, a vile little man with a cobra's temper and brown, beady eyes, was ready too. His uniform was crisp, his creased fatigues as sharp as knives. His boots were mirrors. He stepped into the platoon bay. We stood at attention, foot-lockers and tall lockers open for inspection. The black tile floor glistened from multiple waxings and buffings. Even Roberts, the company drunk standing next to me, looked pretty good. Baer turned to the door frame behind him and ran his white glove across it. It came back clean. He then stepped from man to man, staring each in the eyes for a good fifteen or twenty seconds, looked for twitching, zits, or abnormal behavior. He moved slowly, methodically around the room. We were on the verge of our first weekend leave. We could feel it. We were past hope, approaching conviction that we were gone.

Then he came to Roland Plummer. He found a loosely made bed and a slovenly footlocker. No one had checked out Plummer. Baer tore up the bed and dumped the locker upside down, spilling toiletries, underwear, and socks across the room. "No leaves today," he barked. "I'll be back tomorrow. Get Plummer shaped up, or you won't be going anywhere."

That afternoon, Plummer got a little help from his friends. Half a dozen of the platoon gorillas, including the Montana middle-weight boxing champion, stripped him naked, hauled him into the showers, and scrubbed him down with wire brushes and lye soap. A GI shower, they call it. Plummer squealed like a hog in a slaughterhouse while the guys scrubbed without mercy. The next morning, we passed inspection with flying colors. Roland Plummer was cleaner than most.

Payday came the next week. To collect our monthly pay of $79.20 (11 cents per hour, 24 hours per day, 30 days a month), we had to stand in line while all 250 of us, one at a time, approached Lieutenant Baer, came to attention, saluted, and said, "Private _____ reporting for pay, SIR." We had been trained and retrained that "inferior personnel" do not drop that salute until the ranking officer has dropped his. I practiced mentally holding my salute while Baer scanned me, practiced holding a vacant stare and not flinching or twitching. Word was, he could withhold your pay. Baer looked at me and said, "Which Plummer?"

"Thomas G. Plummer, SIR." I held my salute, tried to keep my hand from shaking.

"Are you related to the *other* Plummer?"

"NO, SIR."

"Well, Plummer," Baer said, speaking slowly and loudly, "you better do something about your namesake. YOU UNDERSTAND?"

He dropped his salute, and I gratefully dropped mine. I'm still not sure what he meant by "namesake." Roland Plummer was not my namesake, but I got the drift. I was also not about to enter into a discussion on the definition of *namesake*.

"YES, SIR."

Every inspection thereafter was terror. Would Roland Plummer be ready? Would he bring punishment down on my head? What would Baer be hollering? "I thought I told you to do something about your namesake, Plummer. Give me twenty one-handed push-ups." Each time Baer inspected the company, each time he stood in front of me with his cobra eyes peeling off my masks, each time I couldn't suppress a twitch, I was sure I was a goner. I needn't have worried. Roland Plummer did not want another GI shower.

Still, I shudder when I hear of other people by the name of Plummer who are out of control. A little twinge of sinless guilt passes through my mind, and Lieutenant Baer's grim words return: "You better do something about your namesake."

I understand why there must be anonymity in the military. It's impossible to imagine an effective combat mission with thousands of individualists doing their thing. Yet deep inside I rebel against anonymity. Kurt Vonnegut Jr. wrote a story in 1961 called "Harrison Bergeron." It's the story of a society in which standing out has become forbidden, and anonymity is the norm. Super ballerinas wear bags of birdshot tied to their legs so they can't leap so high; buzzers go off in people's ears to distract them when they get a particularly bright idea. Harrison Bergeron's society is one of equals. Nobody is different from anyone else: "Nobody is smarter than anybody else. Nobody is better looking than anybody else. Nobody is stronger or quicker than anybody else." A life given to anonymity, to blending in, to disappearing comes close to hiding your light under a bushel. A psychologist friend of mine used to combat sameness. "If we both think alike," he said, "one of us is unnecessary."

On the other hand, once or twice or five or ten times a year or a little more often, I just have to be anonymous for a while. I have to be away from the telephone, from other people, from the knocking at my office door, from e-mail and messages. I have to have an intermission to refuel for the next act. I have to have quiet and solitude. A fly was buzzing in my room one morning. He was so busy, so buzzy, so fly-like, that I had to do him in. I couldn't think. So for a moment I rose out of my self-imposed anonymity and made myself known to him.

Last night there were no lights anywhere. The sky lit up with a carnival of stars. There they were, where they had always been. But we have hidden them behind millions and billions and trillions of artificial lights. When I'm leading a conspicuous life, the stars are obliterated, and when I step back and see them again it's like seeing old friends. And for a few moments I have to envy those people who lived hundreds and thousands of years ago, many of whom led anonymous lives but were able to see the stars most nights.

ON THE VIRTUES
OF PASSION

Looking through my books of quotations under "Passion," I find that it gets a lot of bad press. Passion is a mind out of control. Passion is the absence of reason, sense, sensibility. Passion is what gets you in a lot of trouble. "Appetites, desires, and passions," as a threesome, pose problems. But in the context of "passionately in love," it seems to me, passion makes some sense. I've been in church positions where I interviewed engaged couples. Some of them come in lit up like the sky, happy to be there, happy to be anywhere they're together. They hold hands, they exchange knowing smiles, they fairly twinkle at each other. I ask them why they're getting married, and they say, almost in unison, "Because we're in love." They answer my questions with strong affirmatives; they aren't burdened by anything at all, and this relationship has success stamped all over it.

Other couples come in dazed and dull. They sit a couple of feet away from each other so as not to exchange bacteria; they don't look at each other; they barely look alive. I ask them why they're getting married, and they say, "Oh, well, we're getting older, and it's time to get married."

"How old are you?" I ask.

"Well, she's twenty-one, and I'm twenty-three."

It's marriage by the numbers. I'm old enough, you're old enough, and we might as well get married. I'm deeply concerned in moments like this because, having been married for thirty-seven years, I know that passion can get you through some rough times. You may fight tooth and nail, but a little passion can resolve a lot of nastiness—until you grow up enough in a year or two or fifteen to resolve things with adult conversation.

So when a couple like that comes in, I ask the guy to leave, and I talk to the young woman, who shows all the passion of a mushroom. "Tell me why you want to marry him." I say this with great restraint because I really want to yell, "Run for your life. Just sneak out this back door and get out of here. You've never been in greater danger. Now. Don't look back. Just run."

But I don't say that, so she answers, "Well, I don't know. He's nice."

"Do you love him?" I ask this knowing full well that it's a very complicated question, but I just want to know if there's even any surface love.

"Yeah, I guess so." She shifts in her seat and stares at the floor.

"How long have you known each other?"

"Oh, a month or so."

ON THE VIRTUES OF PASSION

Now, I know there are successful stories of short-term loves. President Spencer W. Kimball's, for one. But he was in love. He felt passion. There was something cooking there.

The interview ends with my deep fear that I have just signed a warrant for eternal unhappiness—or worse, luke-warmness.

In the last few years, I've been more aware of passion—or lack of it—in my own life. Routines set in. My job becomes more predictable, although teaching is never entirely predictable. I start wondering if I'm passionate enough about what I'm doing, or if I've settled for a bland life. Am I just going to get a tumor one day and die? Is that where I'm headed?

In the midst of such gloomy thoughts, one Sunday morning, half-listening to a news program, I heard Charles Kuralt announce, "Coming up, the death of a fly fisherman." It was one of Kuralt's reports from the road. Kuralt was the reporter who drove off in a motor home in the late 1960s to talk to common folk. His reports on the road were so successful that he continued them for more than twenty years. It was not Kuralt the newsman who caught my attention and the attention of millions of other people, it was Kuralt the man who loved people and talked about them in his down-home style, sometimes barely containing his emotions. This was a newsman with a heart. I tried never to miss that program.

I sat up to listen. His report was of Robert Traver, who had just died in his nineties. A video showed him fly fishing on Frenchman's Pond in upper Michigan, his favorite spot in all the world. He was a gray old man in a crumpled hat and full fishing gear, wading slowly, methodically through the misting pond, arching his fly line as delicately as a strand of silk, while Kuralt read Traver's testament of a fly fisherman, which concludes that he fished, "not because I regard fishing as being so terribly important but because I suspect that so many of the other concerns of men are equally unimportant—and not nearly so much fun" *(Trout Magic* [New York: Simon & Schuster, 1974], i).

I rushed to a local bookstore to find out more about Traver. Eventually I found four books he had written, including *Trout Magic* and *Trout Madness: Being a Dissertation on the Symptoms and Pathology of This Incurable Disease by One of Its Victims.* If ever there were essays of passion, they were in these books: Traver struggling for miles through heavy willows and brush with a canoe to reach a new pond; Traver meeting a man on the river and, in a quiet moment, bonding; Traver climbing for hours through backwoods and mountains to a new, isolated fishing spot only to discover that it was on the edge of a major highway.

Piecing together his story, I learned that Traver had been a district attorney on the upper peninsula of Michigan. He kept his fishing gear in the car so that when he traveled around doing D.A. things, he could fish along the way. His law career seemed to be going tolerably well until, when he was about fifty, he lost an election and was unemployed overnight. His practice had been limited to his duties as district attorney, a salaried employee of the state, so he had no private clientele, and he didn't have enough money to retire.

Desperate for cash, he did two things: he took on cases as a criminal defense lawyer, and he began to write a murder mystery, drawing on his experiences as both prosecutor and defender. Doing enough court work to stay afloat, Traver spent every spare minute he had for the next several months writing his mystery about a small-town lawyer-fly-fisherman, Paul Bigler, defending an army officer who has murdered his flirtatious, seductive wife. A formidable prosecutor, Claude Dancer, is brought in from the big city to take the case in behalf of the state. When the book was finished, Traver titled it *Anatomy of a Murder* and sent it to a publisher. He got an immediate rejection. Then another. Eventually St. Martin's Press accepted his book.

About the time it appeared in 1958, the governor of Michigan appointed Traver to the Michigan State Supreme Court, and almost as soon as he assumed his duties in the court, his seat-of-the-pants novel was selected by Book of the Month Club as its featured book. That alone assured a huge windfall, but Traver's luck was just beginning. Otto Preminger, one of Hollywood's most fickle and imperious directors, made the book into a film, which came out in 1959, starring James Stewart as the backwoods lawyer Paul Bigler, Ben Gazzara as Lieutenant Manion, Lee Remick as his wife to be murdered, and George C. Scott as Claude Dancer. Fishing figures heavily into the subplot of both novel and film. In the film, during a meeting in the judge's chambers,

Stewart is fingering a large streamer that he is using as a book mark. The judge asks about it, and the conversation shifts from the trial to fly fishing. Stewart gives the judge the fly, who gratefully accepts it, while George C. Scott looks on in helpless dismay.

When the film was nominated for several Academy Awards in 1959, including Best Picture, Best Actor, Best Supporting Actor, Best Screenplay, and Best Cinematography, Traver had no more worries about money. He quit his job on the Supreme Court and went fishing for the rest of his life, writing a few books, mostly about his adventures in fishing.

I've known other men who were that passionate about fly fishing, but few who found a way to make it their way of life. Maybe one. When I was finishing my undergraduate degree, I met a student who was working on an advanced degree in entomology. His project was to identify and catalogue insects on the Provo River, a blue-ribbon trout stream not far from where we lived. He told me his happiest times were "lab" days on the river, when he could both hunt for insects and go fishing. I don't know what became of him, but I suspect he's a happy man.

It seems to me that people like that have discovered something that eludes many of us: the greatest joy comes from pursuing something you passionately love. The problem, of course, is money. Everyone knows that. So once in a while when we're bored, Louise and I play the "What-would-you-do-if-you-won-the-Publishers-Clearing-House?" game. Questions surface: Would you quit your job? Would you buy a new house? What would you say to people who called asking for money?

And pretty soon it becomes obvious that the problem is not money. If anything, money complicates it all, mucks it up. Money is just another way of enslaving yourself. Money begets obligations and financial advisers and tax agents that I never want to see in my life. Unless your passion is the accumulation of wealth, money gets in the way of it all.

The other problem is that you have to do something more than follow your passion. What about Robert Traver when he wasn't fishing? Was he really so passionate about just one thing that it devoured his whole life? Surely there were other things. Was every morning fishing day? Not on the upper peninsula of Michigan. Not on the cold and snowy days seven months of the year. What about days when the wind chill hit 100 below zero? What did he do then? Did he hang around the house and drive his wife stark raving mad like other retired guys I've heard about? I'd like to hear her side of the story.

What Traver teaches me, however, is humility and passion. Humility that my work is not so earth-shakingly important as I'd like to think. That I'm not going to change the world. That my life will affect at best a few people who will get along just fine after I'm dead. I'm reminded of a time when I thought I was doing big and important stuff, chairing a university department, counseling people at church, spending government money on an arts program. It had all begun to take its toll, because I could see, deep down inside, that it wasn't going to make a lot of difference—except that it was killing me off. A friend, sensing my despair bordering on depression, said, "Tom, if you think you are going to change all these people, you are on a real trip."

But what I truly love about Traver is his unflinching passion for life. He's a man who refused to go down, a man who, when he worked full time, found time for his passion, and when he managed (unlike most of us) to devote full time to his passion, he did so with unparalleled self-awareness and commitment. He devoted himself to a world where the only noise is the song of birds and the sound of a fish rising, where the evening sun reflects clouds off water so still that it's hard to tell the real world from the reflected one. I suspect he died a happy man.

FINDING PATHS
TO AT-ONE-MENT

When Brother Provost first tried to explain the Atonement in my young-adult Sunday School class, I just couldn't wrap my seventeen-year-old mind around it. I don't know that I tried very hard. I was more interested in how I would survive the next weekend's date. The word itself seemed so abstract—even when he broke it down into at-one-ment, the idea of Christ atoning for our sins, making our reconciliation with God possible—that I just gave up. I saw no responsibility of mine in the reconciliation process, as long as I didn't make out with girls, so I just let it fly overhead and be gone. Yes, I understood that I would be reconciled with Father in Heaven if I led a good life; yes, I understood that I had to "do my part." It's just that "my part," whatever that was, was not in my consciousness.

I have to confess that it has not been until recent years that I have begun to rethink the Atonement; that I have felt it take on personal dimensions; that I have realized that it has to do not only with coming together with God but also with finding unity and harmony with other people. "Love one another as I have loved you." That message of oneness, the importance of oneness, the importance of community, the necessity of community did not begin to sink in, quite possibly, until I began to receive dozens of get-well cards and phone calls from current neighbors and friends as well as acquaintances I had not seen for a long time. I was overwhelmed that I mattered that much to them. Clearly they understood better than I the importance of at-one-ment.

Since then I have had moments of lucidity in spite of my spiritual disabilities. When I was serving in a stake presidency several years ago, our regional authority, I'll call him Elder Parsons to protect personal information, held monthly training meetings on Sunday afternoons. Mostly these were business discussions for training purposes. They included statistical reports, reviews of instructions from General Authorities, and special concerns of the people attending. The meetings never spent much time in digression. Elder Parsons was diligent in his work, cut to the business at hand, and stayed there. The busy church officers felt enough pressure from their assignments and absence from families not to waste much time.

On one occasion the agenda shifted for just a few moments, and those few moments have given me several years' worth of things to think about. Elder Parsons began to speak personally. "I've been thinking and reading a lot lately about the Atonement," he said. "That's a central principle of the gospel, and I felt that I didn't understand it as well as I should. I've been reading, studying, and praying about it as time would allow, and this has become an enriching experience. The other day as I studied and prayed, the thought came to me that the Atonement would not be complete for me if I didn't find a way to reconcile with my sister." Here is his account:

My sister had been a difficult child for my parents to raise. She always ran around with the wrong friends, very seldom went to church, and in general began smoking, drinking, and rebelling.

During the years following my mission and marriage we grew far apart. She thought my involvement in the Church and my acceptance of a full-time mission call, which took my family away from home for three years, rather silly. During those three years she called me repeatedly to inform me how upset she was that I would betray our mother by leaving her. My mother died during our absence, and this caused a bigger rift between the two of us because of our decision not to return to attend the funeral. She couldn't understand.

Upon our return, life continued to offer those occasional letters and calls of disgust from her. Finally, after I lectured her on repentance, she became very upset and told me to mind my own business. Actually, I never heard from her again until I realized that in order for me to understand and implement the whole and complete meaning of the Atonement in my life I had to talk to her, ask for her forgiveness, and ask her if there was anything I could do for her. (I would note here, that I was quite close to her in my growing up years prior to my mission and marriage. In fact, following my return from the mission field I baptized each of her three daughters as they reached the age of eight.)

I had to lay the anger and resentment aside. It was impossible for me to receive a full measure of the Atonement without recapturing the harmony and love between us through reconciliation.

I called her. She was living in a nearby state. Her husband answered. When he discovered that I desired to talk to my sister, he said no. I guess he wanted to protect her from additional hard feelings and further anger. After I indicated to him that I wanted to visit with her and ask for her forgiveness, he called her to the phone.

At first she didn't want to talk. I reminded her of the good times we had had in our lives as brother and sister. I told her that I loved her and wanted to ask her forgiveness for the times in her life when I might have offended her. I desired to get things right with her. She started to cry. We had a very pleasant discussion for several minutes and said good-bye.

I felt better. So did she.

Just the other day, I called Elder Parsons on the phone. I told him how I had remembered the story from the meeting and how it had affected me. I explained the project of this book and asked if he would let me retell his story, to which he graciously agreed. To the above he added this information:

I was raised in a so-called dysfunctional family. Both of my parents were born in the covenant. Both sets of their parents passed away early in life, and they were forced into dysfunctional family environments.

FINDING PATHS TO AT-ONE-MENT

Both my parents, a brother, and a sister have died of alcoholism. My brother was married and divorced three times and my sister twice.

I had only one sister living [at the time of the phone call], and she had been married three times and had lived a life of unhappiness for the most part.

It was difficult in this family to connect with the purpose of prayer or a relationship with a Father in Heaven who really cared about you or your family. Because of my upbringing in this family setting, the idea of at-one-ment with those around me, let alone the Savior of the world, was the farthest thing from my mind. Understanding it was one thing. Knowing how it could change lives was another.

A fortunate turn of events came when I was nineteen years of age. Because of the at-one-ment that I felt with special church leaders, I went on a mission. I returned to meet and marry a wonderful woman. Eight children have blessed our union. The encouragement and love of this family has brought me to a meaning and reason for the Atonement. Being "at one" with each of them has been one of the most rewarding blessings of my life.

He then went on to write briefly what had happened since his phone call to his sister and his report in that regional meeting:

Additional calls at the holiday time of the year came around. A year later she passed away with cancer associated with her problems with alcohol. I was asked to take part in the funeral. I traveled to the distant state, paid my respects, and visited with her three daughters. We were able to get many things straightened out.

Several years have passed since that time, but the feeling and spirit that came into my heart through the meaning of the Atonement will never be forgotten.

I can testify of its strength.

Elder Parsons's story moved me to think about the Atonement in personal ways. The picture of him calling a sister from whom he had been alienated and whom he may have hurt, persisting in getting her on the phone when she didn't want to talk to him, and asking her forgiveness—that touches me, because I believe it goes right to the heart of my own role in the Atonement.

I had not asked the question: What do I have to do to understand and implement the whole meaning of the Atonement in my life? With that question, Elder Parsons put himself on the spot. He had to do something. I thought at the time and still think that asking that question was a brave thing to do.

I say that because I fight the idea of taking an active part in my own atonement. I don't really know why. Is it because I'm afraid of too much closeness? Of the burden of closeness with another soul? Am I afraid that connecting, really connecting with someone else will take time away from "more important" things that I have to do? I find it hard to take time for home teaching. I find it hard to respond to heartfelt letters from friends. It's a bit like people who've had heart attacks refusing to diet, even though it might help save their lives.

FINDING PATHS TO AT-ONE-MENT

Maybe I'm cowardly. The spirit of at-one-ment frightens me at times. Is it because I'm shy, because I'm afraid of closeness of the kind Jesus teaches? I've tended to back off at critical times even when I've spent years of closeness with people, people whom I love deeply. Sometimes I wonder if I've got a character flaw. I have backed away or tried to back away from people who have gone out on a limb to reach me.

An Austrian, Ernst Sackl, once wrote to me that I was his best friend. Given his background, I can scarcely imagine what courage he had to summon to make such a declaration. He was in his seventies, I in my twenties. I had been a missionary to him. His wife joined the Church. He lost his courage and did not join, but we remained in contact. He wrote me when his wife died, and through all of this it was clear that we shared spiritual feelings. In a long letter, he said I was his best friend. I had opened his mind to God, he said. He loved me, he said. He wrote in the familiar German "Du," reserved for good friends and family. How could a man in his seventies say I was his best friend? How could I respond to such an unflinching profession of love? What could I say? I wrote nothing. Not a word. I never wrote him back. I don't know when he died, and seldom a week passes that I don't think of Ernst and feel shame for the love I didn't return. I have thought of doing temple work for him, but that is not possible in the scheme of things. I have thought of going back to Köflach, the little coal-mining town where he lived, and finding his grave. I have not done that yet either.

I think Jesus would have written him back. I think Ernst

would have felt His unmistakable love. The story of Ernst reminds me how far short I am of understanding and embracing the Atonement.

I have tried to run at other times and failed. Sometimes I think of it as my Jonah Syndrome. The cover of my first baby album has a gentle, brown leather exterior and a suede interior. Inside and outside are stitched together with a precision leather braiding. The hand-tooled cover frames an oval window that displays a sailboat at full tilt on a stormy sea. My name is engraved in cursive beneath the picture: Thomas Gail Plummer. Uncle Roscoe made that cover. I don't know when. It must be nearly as old as I am. It has graced my baby book all the years I can remember. I cannot open the stories, pictures, and images of my early life without thinking of Roscoe. His gift has intertwined my life with his.

The ship carved into the cover has set a motif for our lives. We have been voyagers together. I first remember Roscoe as a sailor. An early picture shows him with my cousin Frank, my sister Bonnie, and me standing together. And although Roscoe is wearing a white shirt and tie, the caption announces he has been called to serve in the U.S. Navy. The year must be 1943. I don't know who wrote the verse beside the picture, although I strongly suspect my mother:

> Roscoe is going with the Seabees
> To serve his Uncle Sam.
> We don't know where he's going
> Till he sends a telegram.

FINDING PATHS TO AT-ONE-MENT

Everything is so secret
I often wonder why.
We wouldn't tell a single soul.
If we did—I'd hope to die.

A year or so later Roscoe came home on leave between stints building Quonset huts in the Philippines and the Aleutian Islands. There is a picture of the two of us wearing sailor suits. He is kneeling beside me in his Seabees uniform, the dress of the U.S. Navy engineers, and I stand as tall as a five-year-old can, trying to look like a Seabee too. While I am smiling into the camera, Roscoe and our dog, Kelly, are looking at me. We are a threesome. Roscoe is my hero, Kelly our mascot. Maybe, I imagine, I am his hero too. Later, when the war ends, his Seabees shoulder patch will be put in my book of remembrance.

Two letters from Roscoe in the war are also in the book. The first, dated February 16, 1944, reads:

Dear Tommy,

Your mother tells me that you have been such a good boy that I am writing you a letter. We haven't any little boys like you in [then there is a black mark where censors lined out his location] and we surely miss them. The men that live here with me have little boys like you that are good to their mothers and grandmas too. Aunt Ruth and Beth like to talk to you on the telephone. I'll bet Grandma likes to hear you tell stories, doesn't she? When I get home I want to hear you sing and play the piano. If you eat your dinner you will soon be as big as Frank. Then maybe you can ride his bicycle and go sleigh riding. Won't that be fun? Help Grandma and tell Bonnie hello for me. How is old Kelly? Does he still like to bark? Love, Uncle Roscoe.

The second is dated May 4, 1944:

Dear Tommy,

That was a very nice letter you wrote to me. You are surely going to be a smart boy when you start school. When I come home will you read me a long story? Maybe I can tell you about the bear that one of the boys has here. He is a black bear about as big as old Kelly. He likes candy, cake, and things that are sweet. He likes to play with the boys. When you give him a candy bar he stands up on his hind feet to get it. The man that owns him is going to take him home with him on the ship. Be a good boy. Love, Roscoe.

One thing I love about these letters is Roscoe's connection with everyone in the family. While he is writing to me, he shows me a sense of how everyone matters and should matter to me—Mother, Aunt Ruth, Aunt Beth, Grandma,

Frank, Bonnie, even Kelly the dog. It was a role I believe Roscoe must always have played in the family. He connected the group, somehow brought them together.

When the war ended, Roscoe came to live with my family for a year or so. His life and mine were spent in daily intersections. We gave each other nicknames. He named me "Rabbit," referring to the tale of "The Tortoise and the Hare" and how the hare lost the race by running in spurts rather than by being consistent. In retaliation, I began calling him "Turtle." Those names stuck to the very end. Roscoe rarely greeted me with anything but "Hello, Rabbit." I would reply, "Hi, Turtle." I have since learned that 1939, the year I was born, was the Chinese year of the rabbit, and of all the animals in the Chinese mythology, the rabbit is luckiest. So I am grateful to Roscoe for attaching a lucky label to me.

Why, then, was it so hard to respond when Roscoe needed me? He lay in the hospital, seriously ill, and someone from the family called to say I needed to visit him. "He's very depressed," the caller said. I was busy and thought I would go when the time was convenient. When that call came, I knew that it was my responsibility to give Roscoe a blessing. It was just a feeling. No one said it. But I knew it. I knew that Roscoe needed me.

Still, for a day or two, I pulled back. I stalled. At-onement seemed awkward and a little frightening, even with this uncle who had given so much of himself to me. I had not seen him depressed before. Was it possible that he was really depressed? My sister called, then her son called to say Roscoe needed a blessing. I got hold of myself and went with my son Charles. Roscoe lay in his hospital bed, tubes, it seemed, running in and out of his body from everywhere. He held out his hand. "Hello, Rabbit."

"Hello, Turtle. You seem to be on your back."

"Yes." He looked at me with deep and sad eyes. It seemed to me I could see in them generations of ancestors. I saw the eyes of my grandmother, who died while I was a missionary. The eyes of my grandfather, who died two years before I was born. The eyes of countless generations past, of Warnocks and McIntyres and Swindles. They all converged in Roscoe's eyes.

"We've come to give you a blessing, Ross," I said.

"Oh, I don't know if I should have a blessing," he said. "I've disappointed my family. I don't seem to be getting along too well at church."

We talked for a long time about church and family. He talked about how important his assignment as a home teaching supervisor was to him, how much certain men meant to him. He talked about how he loved his sisters, and how sad he was that he couldn't do more for them. He talked about his wife and son and his love for family. Then he said, "If you think I should have a blessing, I'd like to have it now."

As I laid my hands on him, I knew God loved him. I have often had that feeling in giving blessings. It comes to me, and I suspect to others, as a deep, unmistakable tingling that abides throughout the blessing and then quietly leaves.

Recently I went to visit Roscoe's older sister, my Aunt Ruth, a woman who always said she wanted to die with a fishing pole in her hand. She'd had a stroke. She'd fallen and broken her hip. She was miserable beyond words, and she was dying. I asked her if there was anything I could do for her. She said, "Pray for me." I asked if she would like a blessing. She said, "Yes. I want to rest." I laid my hands on her head, and in the moment I did that, I realized her head was the same shape as my mother's. It was as if I were giving my own mother a blessing, only Aunt Ruth's head was still warm, my mother's cold now. But for just a moment I was able to touch my mother once more. In retrospect, it was very much like the experience of blessing Roscoe and coming in touch with those who had passed on. I was so overcome, I couldn't speak for quite a while. Louise said she opened her eyes to see what was going on. Aunt Ruth has always been very unlike my mother in her personality. But in that moment, with my hands on her head, with my hands on my mother's head, with my hands on the link to long-past generations, I was overwhelmed with their oneness, and I knew that God loved Aunt Ruth and that I loved her deeply. In that moment, Aunt Ruth and Mother and I reached a new level of at-one-ment.

And so I struggle to understand, to realize the great and profound blessings of at-one-ment, and know that I will always struggle to embrace it fully. I get off center so easily. My spiritual consciousness dissipates like drops of water hitting a hot pan, sometimes so quickly that I'm astonished at my own shallowness.

When I'm removed from at-one-ment, when I am spiritually off center, I start bustling in obsessive ways—opening and shutting drawers, rushing around the house giving orders. I drive badly and mutter a lot about other people's incompetence. Fortunately, Louise has become an astute observer of this behavior and knows how to calm me down. If she's not holding a hammer, the scriptures will do. On one of those off-center days, when I was getting on her nerves, she finally said, "Stop. You're being very ungrateful. We've just had miracles happen, and you're acting like God isn't in your life. We're going to stop right now and read some scriptures. Sit down here on the bed."

I sat down dutifully on the bed. Louise picked up her scriptures and said, "Okay, what do you want to hear? I'll read."

Being in the wrong frame of mind in the first place, I had to think for a minute or two. She waited patiently.

"How about the great intercessory prayer in John 17," I said. I wanted to listen to Jesus pray.

Louise began reading. It was like listening to a serenade, Jesus almost singing his prayer to the Father: "Neither pray I for these alone, but for them also which shall believe on me through their word; that they all may be one; as thou, Father, art in me, and I in thee, that they also may be one in us: that the world may believe that thou hast sent me. And the glory which thou gavest me I have given them; that they may be one, even as we are one: I in them, and thou in me, that they may be made perfect in one; and that the world may know that thou hast sent me, and hast loved them, as thou hast loved me" (John 17:20–23). Surely nothing in all of scripture or literature is more beautiful than those words; nothing shows in more intricate and simple language the beauty of at-one-ment. And for a little while again I am at one—with God, with his children, with myself. By God's grace, I'm at one.

CHRIST'S LOVE
FOR EACH PERSON

I wonder if any other word in the English language is more used and less understood than *love*. As most of us learned in school, the ancient Greeks distinguished between platonic and erotic love. A school of child rearing emerged a few years ago with the motto "tough love." Thoughts on love take up fifty-four pages in my *Home Book of Quotations,* ranging from attempts at definitions to a search for causes (biologists now have some thoughts on the chemistry of love) to ideas about love and fear. All of this has proven to be of little practical use to me in understanding what love is and what I am to make of this barrage in my daily life. Is my love for my wife, for example, erotic, platonic, tough, or all three, and in what balance? Can I say that my love for my parents is platonic, and how then would I distinguish between platonic love for my parents and, say, platonic love for a friend?

And when we speak of young people being in love, I wonder, as many mature readers likely do, if we are not confusing love with lust. It may be more accurate to say they are "in lust." We speak of the madness of love. We speak of love's follies. We speak of blind love as Shakespeare did in his Sonnet 137:

Thou blind fool, Love, what does thou to mine eyes,
That they behold and see not what they see?

The noted American psychologist Carl Rogers tackles the question of love in human relationships in his book *Becoming Partners.* He explores several definitions of love, ruling one or the other out for well-founded reasons, and finally concludes that to love is to commit yourself to the growth of another person. Rogers's definition makes more sense to me than any I have read before or since. It reverses the notion that I had as a young man looking for a wife: love is attaching yourself to someone who will commit herself to your growth. Wrong. Love is committing yourself to the growth of another.

I've been thinking a great deal lately about Christ's love. When I think about His love, my mind always drifts to two scriptures:

John 3:16: "For God so loved the world, that he gave his only begotten Son, that whosoever believeth in him should not perish, but have everlasting life."

John 13:34: "A new commandment I give unto you, That ye love one another; as I have loved you, that ye also love one another."

It seems to me that the Lord defines love in about the same way as Rogers did: The purpose of God's love is to ensure our everlasting life. He intends for us to accomplish the full measure of our creation, and in order for us to do that, he has sacrificed his Son for our salvation. He wants us to grow and develop into full and complete human beings, and then to realize our divine potential. It is a corollary to this commitment that we have agency. Without agency, how can we fulfill the measure of our personal creation? Our eternal growth is highly individual and personal, and our accomplice in this is God himself.

This is a staggering thought for many, who have grown up thinking they have only to follow others, that they have no divine potential, no great worth of their own, that they have been weighed in the balance and found wanting. Human beings have invented numerous ways of convincing each other of this. In universities, we have admissions exams that cut some people out and let others in. We have grades that tell students how they stack up. In later years we talk of net worth and political power, as if any of these—scores, grades, wealth, or power—have anything much to do with our worth in the eyes of God. These are all artificial instruments that we have created to judge each other. They are most certainly not God's measures.

One of my colleagues, a professor, grew up in a household that valued high academic standards. Fortunately for him, his gifts were academic in nature, and he was able to meet the expectations that his parents held for him. He married a woman whose academic standards were just as high as his. Surely, they thought, they would raise children who shared those abilities and those standards. They were wrong. Their children have not followed in their footsteps, and the parents have learned, ever so slowly over the years, that they were blessed, not cursed, with children who have their own gifts.

Their fourth daughter, Jennifer, they worried, might even have some learning disabilities. She was slow in speech, slow in reading, and a lousy speller. They shook their heads in dismay as they read her little papers in grade school that denied the probability of a scholar in the making. What would become of her? they wondered. How would she make her way in the world? Her fifth-grade teacher shared these worries, especially since he had had one of her sisters a few years before who was quite gifted with language.

The teacher told Jennifer one day that she should ask her parents to have her tested. Jennifer came home from school crying, knowing full well that her teacher thought that she was "stupid." "Stupid" was Jennifer's word, not the teacher's, but she got the drift. Her parents arranged for testing at a nearby university, but the earliest date they could get was several months away. The teacher became impatient. One day during an oral reading session in class, as Jennifer was struggling along, the teacher asked in a loud voice in front of the class, "Jennifer, have your parents had you tested yet?" Jennifer was devastated and again came home crying. The parents were sure the tests would show her to be learning disabled.

The day finally came, and the tests took several hours,

including written exercises and conversation with examiners. The parents sat nervously in the waiting room. From time to time they could hear Jennifer and the examiners laughing. The atmosphere was obviously pleasant, even jovial. Finally the examiner came out to discuss the findings with the parents. He got right to the point. "The only problem Jennifer has," he said, "are the adults in her life."

He pointed out that Jennifer was aware of some difficulties with language but had developed rather ingenious ways of working through and around them. He discussed newer studies of intelligence that consider human capacities much more broadly than IQ tests and suggested that precisely because Jennifer was not a superstar in ways the parents were accustomed to thinking of superstars, they now had an opportunity to learn about her unique abilities that maybe, just maybe they didn't have. The implication was that if someone had created a test to measure the parents by Jennifer's abilities, they would flunk it cold.

They backed off and told her teacher to do the same. Before long they noticed that Jennifer had strong social skills (much stronger than those of her parents), as well as strong intuitive skills. Consistent with Jennifer's perceptual skills have come spiritual gifts that the parents can only admire from a distance. In the end, it has not been Jennifer who needed to upgrade her intellectual skills but her parents who needed to upgrade their emotional skills.

If we believe in a law of eternal progression, then we must believe that the purpose of a family, and the purpose of

Christ's church, is to discover the gifts of each of its members and to help each one achieve his or her potential—not as we perceive that potential to be but as the divine gifts that person has.

This is not always easy. Some of our closest friends, Mike and Shirley, have had a son who has struggled greatly to come to terms with himself, with the family, and with God. There have been times, they've told us, when they wanted to give up.

When Patrick approached missionary age, they talked to their bishop and advised him not to discuss a mission with Patrick. "It just won't work for him," they said. "He won't get along with companions, and he won't get along with members and investigators in the mission field. Give him other assignments, things he can do at home, but don't even think about calling him on a mission." He agreed.

But when Patrick turned nineteen, he went to the bishop and said he wanted to go on a mission. The bishop called Mike. "What do you want me to do?" he asked.

"Treat him like any other prospective missionary," he said. "If he is worthy and wants to serve, he should go. But I'm worried."

"Yeah, me too," the bishop said.

When the call came, Patrick did not want it. It was for the Georgia Atlanta Mission. He wanted Australia. He checked out three R-rated movies and spent the day sequestered in his room watching them. The next morning was Sunday. He came out of his room dressed for church and said he was sorry, that he was ready to go on his mission.

He went, but after eleven months of failed companionships and misery, he decided he'd had enough. In spite of difficulties, he was on good terms with his mission president, who encouraged him to stay. It was not to be. He called his parents on a Thursday and said he was coming home Saturday.

Mike made a last-ditch effort to convince him not to come home, as had his mission president. "I don't remember what I said," he told me. "I hope it was something like, 'This may be the saddest decision of your life. Please reconsider.' More likely I said something stupid, like offering a homespun psychoanalysis of his problems."

Patrick took offense and said, "Well, if you really want to know the truth, I'm just coming home to get my things, change my name, get excommunicated, and move to Florida. I don't want you to meet me at the airport. I don't want to see you again." He hung up, and they had no idea how to call him back. This was Thursday. They knew only that his plane was arriving two days later, on Saturday.

"We've lost him," Mike said as he hung up. He and Shirley sat together stunned.

"I prayed that day as earnestly as I've ever prayed for anything," Mike told me. How could he turn this around? How could he save this son, whom he had tried to save so many times before? Was this the end?

"I was half-sleeping, half-dreaming the next morning,

Friday, about three A.M.," he said. "I became aware of a presence, not a being or a heavenly messenger, but a spiritual power over my head, and the words came clearly to mind, 'You must love this boy.' It hit me with such force and clarity that I knew almost immediately what had to be done."

He woke Shirley and told her what had happened and exactly what he thought they needed to do.

"Yes, that is right," she said.

As soon as daybreak came, Mike called members of the family to a special meeting and told them what had happened. He called Shirley's parents and brothers and sisters. He called his mother, who was as close to Patrick as anyone, and told her. He called his sister in a distant state, whom Patrick loved, and told her.

"I'm coming on the next plane," she said.

In the meeting Mike told them all, "Patrick doesn't want Shirley and me to meet him at the airport. So we'd like the three grandparents and my sister, Elizabeth, to meet him. He loves the four of you, and we don't think he will be able to reject you. He's mad at us, but he's not mad at you. We'd like the rest of you—Shirley's brothers, sisters, spouses, children—to come down to our home and wait for them to arrive there. All we want you to do is hug him, welcome him home, and leave. Just let him know he's loved."

One of Shirley's brothers, an air traffic controller, was not at the meeting because he had to work. He devised his own plan. He was on duty when Patrick's plane came in. As the plane approached Salt Lake, he radioed the captain about an Elder Patrick Matthews.

As Patrick later related it, the captain came on the loudspeaker. "We'd like to welcome Elder Patrick Matthews home from his mission in Atlanta, Georgia. Congratulations, Elder Matthews."

"The captain had a low voice like Dad's," Patrick said. "I thought it was Dad. I thought, 'My gosh, I can't get away from my dad.'"

When Patrick entered the terminal, the three women—two grandmothers and an aunt—rushed him, kissed him, hugged him, and told him they loved him. He melted down. His grandfather hugged him and helped him get his luggage, and the five of them headed for Spanish Fork. It was the day of a BYU football game, and they got stuck in game traffic. They were on the highway for nearly two hours. By the time they reached home, they had thoroughly warmed up to each other.

Shirley's siblings and their families were waiting when the car pulled in. They opened the doors, dragged Patrick out, smothered him with more hugs, and turned him over to Shirley and Mike. The fight was over. They hugged each other, cried a bit, and began the long process of getting on with the rest of their lives. That afternoon the bishop called Patrick from the airport—he was going out of town—and welcomed him home.

Later that evening, the stake president came to the house to talk to Patrick and to release him. "You know, Patrick," he said, "eleven months of a mission for one person may be like five years for another."

"What has happened to Patrick?" I asked my colleague recently.

"Oh, he has struggled on and off. He's had an unsuccessful marriage, but things are looking up for him. He's taking responsibility for his life, he's owning his differences with the family and accepting them, and he seems to have found a lovely girl who understands his rough edges. He has work. He works hard. He's going to be all right."

If I've learned anything from watching Patrick, it is this: Christ does not give up easily. He allows our errors, loves us still, even takes our rebukes, and then, when we are ready, he reaches out, lifts us up, and gives us peace. Perhaps the hard part of knowing that Christ loves us for the people we are is the other adults in our lives who send messages that maybe there's something wrong with us. Our job is to learn to ignore the interference and accept Christ's love.

THE BLESSINGS
OF UNCERTAINTY

As more and more of my friends become ill and feeble, I wrestle more with questions of life's uncertainty. Again and again I'm appalled that this friend or that friend, this marathoner or that diet watcher has fallen. I wonder how it is possible, how it can be explained. And again and again I am drawn to a few lines from Moses, chapter 4, in the Pearl of Great Price. The Council in Heaven is under way, and God the Father is discussing how his children will return to him once their time on earth has passed. Satan and Jesus each put forward a plan. Satan says that he will see that we all behave as we should and will insure that we all return to God. No one will be lost. In his words, "I will redeem all mankind, that one soul shall not be lost, and *surely* I will do it." The Father rejects Satan's plan, probably for two reasons: first because Satan wants to take all glory for his accomplishment, and second because, the scripture says, he "sought to destroy the agency of man" (Moses 4:1, 3; emphasis added).

It's the one short phrase, "surely I will do it," that catches my attention. "*Surely* I will do it." This is a debate on the subject of certainty and uncertainty. Certainty, coupled with our loss of freedom, is Satan's plan. Uncertainty, coupled with agency, is the Father's plan, which is a simple plan on the surface. But beneath it are complications that leave us struggling.

Satan's plan—no one will be lost—has a seductive appeal. "Surely I will do it," he says. If, in raising my children, I knew that not one would be lost, if I knew what tomorrow brought, if I knew that their eternal salvation were secured, it might be easier. There would be no violence; there would be no alcohol; there would be no adultery. It sounds almost good.

I sometimes wonder if I anticipated then, in that preexistent time, if I foresaw clearly that agency brought with it a whole lot of uncertainty, uncertainty that I often would much rather avoid. It is uncertainty that puts agency to the test; it is uncertainty that leaves me baffled at the misfortune of all humankind. When push comes to shove, I'd often like God to take care of things for me. I'd like God to fix my messes. It's the cowardly side of me. But no. I have agency, and nothing is sure.

It doesn't have to be big calamities that upset me. Little, unforeseen disasters abound. There are just not enough ways to secure myself. Like the night I was driving on a section of freeway under construction. All but two lanes were walled off with concrete. I was passing the car alongside me, when I looked ahead to see a large steel pipe rolling toward my car. A steel pipe rolling down the freeway. There was no place to go. To the left was concrete, to the right was the other car. So I drove over the pipe. There was a bang underneath, but the car kept moving. When I got home, I could smell oil, and when I checked the rear of the car, it was covered with an oily substance. The pipe had wiped out my rear transaxle, which my insurance company paid $2,500 to fix and then cancelled my policy, claiming it was an "at-fault accident."

Something similarly unexpected happened to my friend Lorin one night over dinner at Helen's Restaurant. Lorin, Judy, Louise, and I were enjoying a pleasant meal when Lorin jerked and grabbed his thigh like a crocodile had just locked onto him. He had what I've always called a charley horse, only he had a charley Man O' War.

My fax to him at his office later on sort of expresses my regret:

> Dear Lorin,
>
> I have been greatly concerned about you since the sudden muscle spasm in your thigh at Helen's Restaurant the other night, when your leg developed an ostrich-sized egg and you hobbled out to walk it off. I'm sorry for accusing you of trying to avoid paying your share of the bill. I suppose it's something I might do myself, and I realized later, I was just projecting my own deviance on you.
>
> Because you are a good friend, because I feel sorry that I accused you unjustly, and because I

feel badly that you are obviously showing the same signs of aging as the rest of us, I have done some research to make up for my bad behavior. I got out my Johns Hopkins *Symptoms and Remedies* and looked up possible causes of your cramping. As you can see, I've attached copies of pages 200 ("Muscle cramps"), 201 ("Muscle spasms"), and 202 ("Muscle spasticity"). Peruse them at your leisure. They pair off symptoms with possible diagnoses.

I know you are a busy man, since you are not a professor, so I offer my own analysis of those sheets, which may be quicker for you. I think we can rule some things out right away: any of the ailments with distinguishing features like speaking difficulty, involuntary crying, and drooling. I saw no such symptoms, although I noticed that you whimpered as you hobbled out of the restaurant, dropped a bit of the halibut with the baked hazelnut crust on your shirt, and dribbled diet Coke down your chin. I thought that may have been caused by an ice cube causing a jam as the drink passed through your teeth. I did notice you were tipping the glass a bit steeply, but I thought, "Hey, Lorin knows what he's doing, let him do it his way." Should I have intervened?

I would also rule out any illness with such

symptoms as hair loss, unless you've bought a
toupee recently; itching (just because you said
nothing about it—did you have violent itching
accompanying the spasm?); and puffiness
around the eyes. I attributed the bags under
your eyes to normal signs of aging.

I considered rabies for a few moments, but
dropped the idea because your behavior, while
just as obnoxious as mine, involved no loss of
appetite and no violence.

This, I'm afraid, all leads me to the conclu-
sion that my doctors often reach: I just don't
know what's wrong with you. Probably some
long-term degenerative ailment. You'll live for
another five years, no sweat.

Best,
Tom

Sometimes we blame God for our uncertainty. I know a
man who is angry with God because God hasn't made his life
better for him. He thinks he should be married, so he makes
bad choices in marrying and then is angry with God when
the marriage fails. Why, this man asked me, did God let the
marriage fail? How can God stand by and let things like that
happen? My reply is always the same. God won't prevent fail-
ures, even if they hurt you, because God has made it clear
that we have agency. He may give support if we ask him,
although possibly not the support we asked for, but he will

not step in to break up a failure like a referee breaking up a brawl in the ring. If God interfered every time we made a mess of our lives, we would stand around waiting for him to tell us our next step or waiting for lightning to stop us from doing dumb things. My friend is unconvinced.

There is a cancer that spreads through our culture. I see it often among my students, a belief that if you are obedient, you will never have problems. You'll marry the right person, have lovely, tractable children, never see serious problems or illness, and die in the twinkling of an eye. It's a dream of a life of happiness ever after, a fairy tale. All you have to do is obey. It is a dream that overlooks entirely the scripture that admonishes us that there must be opposition in all things. Sorrow brings a greater appreciation of joy; grief brings compassion for others who grieve. We cannot live our lives with that beautiful white smile that gorgeous people wear on our television screens after they have used their Colgate toothpaste. Many have come to expect a life without seams, a life without sickness and sorrow. We expect a life of certainty. We want Satan's plan.

If we lived that fairy tale, my father-in-law would not have died the death he died last year. He would have been translated into eternal life sometime last spring. The fact is, however, Louis died a slow, agonizing death. He had a neurological condition that doctors diagnosed as a basal ganglionic degeneration. I don't pretend to know anything about the pathology of the disease. I only know it as I witnessed its evolution. When Louis visited us a year ago July in Nova

Scotia, he was full of energy, full of ideas about travel and adventure that were hindered only by his wife's Alzheimer's. This frustrated him no end because not only would she no longer travel with him, she could no longer talk with him about their former lives and adventures together, their life during the war in Holland, the births of their nine children, their missions to Holland and Switzerland. She doesn't remember the day they married. She doesn't remember their intimate moments, and now she barely speaks at all. His frustration took up the first two days of conversation during his visit as he muttered again and again, "She has no memory; she has no life. She has no memory; she has no life."

It was then that we noticed the onset of his own illness, ever so subtle, like a tiny spring that seeps from the ground to become a river miles downstream. He complained as we walked along the beach that his legs felt rubbery, that he didn't feel too sure of his gait. I noticed just a little foot drop as he walked. Twice, as he climbed over uneven rocks, he slipped and fell but jumped right back up. We thought no more of it. On the way home, he missed a connecting flight in Boston and spent the day strolling around Logan Airport. We didn't know this until relatives who were to pick him up in Salt Lake called and asked if he'd left Nova Scotia. We were finally able to learn from airline service people that he would be on the next flight to Salt Lake, which left in a few hours. We worried that he couldn't take care of himself, but that turned out to be untrue. When he got home, he told everyone how he had enjoyed spending time alone again, and how good it felt to know he could still be independent, walking around the airport, doing as he pleased.

By the time we arrived home, one month later, things had deteriorated. He was losing his balance and falling more often; he was becoming disoriented; and it was clear to the family, although it was not yet clear to him, that he could never again spend a day alone.

Not many months later, when Louise and I visited her parents at the care center, her father, a mere fragment of his former self, sat slumped over in a wheelchair, while her mother, whose Alzheimer's had worsened, sat silently and wheeled his chair gently back and forth as if she were rocking a baby.

Could one assume that God has inflicted this upon them? Could one assume they were experiencing the consequences of a life badly lived? This couple was married fifty-nine years. They raised eight children, all of whom, Louis was proud of saying, married and were sealed to their spouses in the temple. Louis served for a total of twelve years as a bishop, ten years as stake president, and three or four years as stake patriarch. He and his wife served two missions and many years as temple workers. Was God punishing them? Who can say with certainty why they have suffered?

And who would dare to explain the death of young Michael Johnson one late-autumn Saturday in Minnesota? Early that morning, our phone rang. The voice on the other end said, "Bishop Plummer, this is Marie Johnson."

"Well, good morning, Marie," I said in my most cheerful

voice. I seldom heard from Marie. Marie came to church regularly, taught Primary and attended sacrament meeting, then slipped out quietly when meetings were over. I knew about her family, about their struggles, but she had come to talk about them only once, to get a referral for family counseling. Jim, her husband, was an alcoholic, and his drinking had become a destructive force in the family that had taken him and their children pretty much out of the Church. Once in a great while, Jim would come to church, but although he was friendly, he avoided making any more than casual contact with me or any other members of the ward. I saw their children rarely.

Marie's voice that Saturday morning was flat and unemotional. "Michael died in a deer hunting accident this morning," she said. Michael was their oldest child. He was nineteen. In the same monotone, Marie said that Michael had gone hunting near Pipestone, Minnesota, with his cousin. When they arrived at their spot, Michael grabbed his deer rifle out of the truck and jogged down the trail. Jerry, his cousin, grabbed his rifle, closed up the truck, and started running after Michael. He had not checked the safety on his rifle. When he stumbled on a root, the gun went off. The bullet hit Michael in the back of the head and killed him instantly.

"I'll come right over," I said.

"Yes, I'd like that," Marie said.

By the time I arrived, the house was full of relatives. Most of them lived nearby and had come as soon as the news of Michael's death spread. I hugged the parents, who were still numb from the whole thing, and expressed my sadness. I asked what had happened to Jerry, the cousin.

"He's over there in the corner," Marie said.

Jerry sat in the corner, looking pale and anesthetized. I went over to him, introduced myself, and put my arm around him. It was, to my knowledge, the first time anyone had touched him since the accident. He leaned into me and began to talk. He talked about planning the hunt, about seeing Michael drop in his tracks on the trail. I asked him about the family. He said some were mad at him, that Michael's girlfriend, who was seventeen years old, had accused him of killing Michael so he could have her.

We talked for a long time. My intention, insofar as possible, was to let Jerry know that I knew, and I was sure Michael knew, that he had not killed him on purpose. It was an accident. It was a terrible accident.

I next saw Jerry at the funeral. While other family members wept together and hugged each other, Jerry sat alone at the end of a bench. After the service, I waited for him at the door of the funeral chapel. Everyone had left to go to their cars. The casket was gone. Jerry sat in the chapel, stunned and very much alone. Finally he stood up to leave. As he came down the aisle toward me, I opened my arms, and he fell into them sobbing. It was the last time I ever saw him.

About two weeks after the funeral, Jim, Michael's father, called. His voice was agitated. "Bishop," he said, "why did Michael die?"

I had not anticipated his call or his question, but my

answer came quickly. "Jim," I said, "Michael died because he got hit in the back of the head with a bullet from a deer rifle. That will kill you every time."

"You don't think God called him home?" he asked.

"No," I said. "He died an accidental death, pure and simple."

"Oh, thank goodness," he said. "People have been telling me God must have called him home to serve a mission on the other side. Some said he was too good for this world. And I've been telling myself that if I'd been active, I would have been taking him to church and he wouldn't have gone deer hunting."

I wondered if any church authority would agree with what I had told Jim. Had Michael been called "home" to serve the mission that he wasn't going to serve here? I was relieved, a month or two later, to come across an article by President Spencer W. Kimball in the *Ensign* that said the same thing I had told Jim, that accidents happen that cut our lives short, and that's part of the chance we take in coming to earth. Life is a risk. It involves uncertainty of all kinds.

With all the heartaches that come with agency, the plan that removes certainty from our lives, we might come to see it as a curse. We might wonder if it serves any good purpose and set out on our own plan to control ourselves and others. Totalitarian governments try it all the time.

With all of its accompanying trouble, I choose agency. Uncertainty is the beginning of hope. It necessitates hope. It is the beginning of faith. It necessitates faith. Uncertainty leaves us dependent on the Comforter. When we agreed to come to this earth, we agreed to take on not only happiness and joy, not only the Garden of Eden, but also the hardships of life, its sorrow, its grief, its pain. We could not stay in Paradise. Like Adam and Eve in Milton's *Paradise Lost,* we've entered a solitary world:

> The World was all before them, where to choose
> Their place of rest, and Providence their guide:
> They hand in hand with wand'ring steps and slow,
> Through EDEN took their solitary way.

Some of us got more hardship than others, but I think that before life is over, the great majority of us will have undergone suffering of a great enough intensity that we might have been tempted to skip the whole deal and stay with Father in Heaven if we could have foreseen it clearly enough. But he, in his wisdom, said we had to learn hope, and faith, and charity, which could not come from Satan's plan, because faith and hope and even charity are not necessary when salvation is a done deal.

The events of September 11, 2001, and December 7, 1941, would give us cause to wonder about the blessings of uncertainty. Do blessings really come with uncertainty? Our assumptions about national security, our assumptions about our very safety in going to work, opening the mail, or flying in an airplane have all been called into question. How are we safe? Can our national leaders protect us? Can our church leaders ensure our safety? The fact is, uncertainty will defy any amount of security. We may reduce uncertainty by tightening security, but we will never eliminate it. I cringe when I hear anyone in a position of authority assure us that we are safe.

Even in the face of uncertainty, I am glad for agency, for choice, for a loving Father who watches over me and blesses me but does not intervene in my struggles. I am grateful for his quiet promptings when I listen. Sometimes I wish they were a little louder, so I could be more certain of them, but then, on reflection, I'm not so sure.

THE STRUGGLE
FOR SOLITUDE

The idea, even the idea of solitude has been tough for me. I suspect my reluctance goes back to childhood. In fourth grade I became terrified that my mother would leave. I had never heard my parents fight, and I never actually thought of her leaving my father. I had never been abandoned. I just feared that when I came home from school she would be gone. I have no idea what gave rise to this anxiety, a deep, existential *Angst* that by the end of the day my mother, the lynchpin of my sanity, would disappear, and I would be alone in the world.

It was not the case that my mother was invisible. I remember few days when she was not home after school, and when she wasn't, my grandmother was there. But my grandmother was old and feeble, and if my mother left the scene, Grandma could not pick up the slack. Dad, I must have figured, was always at work and wouldn't be around to take care of me. I would be alone, as alone as Max with the Wild Things.

And so it was that before going to school each day, I would ask Mother if she was going to be there when I got home. She always said that she would. I would then make myself ready, gather lunch and books or whatever I needed, and ask her again if she was going to be home. Yes, she would say. I would get to the front door, turn around, and ask again. And sometimes I'd return after a few steps, open the door, and ask again. Even as I write, I can feel the pulsations, the energy my whole body put into this obsession. It was more than a thing in my head. I could feel it physically straining my arms and legs, an antsy creeping up and down my spine. *Go back and ask again*, it told me. I would go back and ask just one more time. And again. And again.

I suppose this would now be diagnosed as an obsessive-compulsive disorder. I would get some pills and be done with it. But it wasn't so simple back in the 1940s. My sister once told me during those days that Mom and Dad were worried about me. I was sorry, but I felt completely helpless to change.

Finally my parents took me to a child psychologist. This I considered tantamount to being declared insane. I had had no traffic with psychologists before, and I knew no adults who were psychologists, but I knew that psychologists dealt with people who were mentally ill. I recoiled when I saw him, although he was a kind enough man. He introduced me into a room filled with toys. It took but a glance to see how artificial it all was. I was supposed to sit in this play room with a man I'd never met and have a conversation. I was supposed to play with his toys, and he would watch me and figure out just how nuts I really was.

So I wouldn't play with the toys. Even at his urging, I wouldn't pick one up. It was a conspiracy. I wouldn't answer his questions, either. I was an uncooperative little stink, as my mother might have said. I just wasn't going to get into this mental thing. After a few fruitless visits, he had a consultation with me and my parents. He told me I needed to get more sleep.

Even at that age, I knew that he had failed, and I knew that he knew it. I really didn't care. He had his problems; I had mine. The episodes continued for another year or so. I felt depressed and anxious during that time, but nothing more was to be done. Now I think of a joke a psychologist friend told me: How many psychologists does it take to change a light bulb? Answer: just one, but it's really gotta want to change. I wasn't going to change, and a thousand psychologists weren't going to make any difference. Eventually I matured and the whole thing went away.

More or less. There has been a residual anxiety deep down in my gut about being alone. I don't take to it naturally. So when people talk about the virtues of solitude, I have to get a grip on myself, remembering that solitude means being alone but not necessarily isolated or lonesome, that it's a constructive thing.

On the other hand, I have had to face the curious fact that although I don't care to be alone, I am an introvert. I know this because I took some personality tests that say I'm an introvert. As a matter of fact, I took the Myers-Briggs test twenty years ago, which showed me to be mildly introverted. When I took it again on the Internet recently, it showed me to be much more introverted. Over the years I have moved further and further into the introverted side, which means my primary source of energy is from the inner world of thoughts and emotions rather from the outer world of activity and spoken words. After a hard day in the working world, introverts don't go looking for a cocktail party to recharge their batteries. They seek solitude.

I learned recently that people of my ilk constitute less than 5 percent of the population. I can meet others like me by attending the post-Christmas meetings of the Modern Language Association, although I hate to admit it. There I see thousands of men with beards, wearing tweed jackets and Hush Puppies, and carrying their coffee in foam cups, which they hold with spindly fingers. Though I don't have a beard, wear Hush Puppies, or drink coffee, I am one of them, I guess.

Not surprisingly, introverts get bad press. Society has pinned labels on the most extreme of them, implying that they are social misfits. Guys are referred to as loners, lone wolves, hermits, or, to a lesser degree, bookworms, nerds, and pantywaists. I don't know the derogatory terms for women introverts.

So I am an introvert with residual anxieties about being alone. It has taken no small effort to span this chasm in my personality and to accept that solitude has both virtues and rewards. I take comfort from the writing of William Penn, who in his late years wrote a treatise called "Some Fruits of Solitude." His opening sentence calls solitude "a school few care to learn in, tho' None Instructs us better." Penn's treatise then goes on to explore his life, his values—education, charity, discipline, industry—and his disdain for ignorance, murmuring, and criticism of others. The implication, given his premise, is that without solitude, he would not be able to reflect so earnestly or well about his life.

Solitude is the source of wisdom about oneself, the Taoist says, because the Self is anchored in God (the Tao) and only in solitude do we find God. The direction of modern society is toward false gods, which we serve in abundance. Only in serving the real God, the Taoist implies, do I attain freedom, which is possible only as I come to know myself. Only in solitude is all of this harmony with God possible. The task is to stay centered in God.

The further I am from solitude, the further I am from God and, consequently, from self. Happiness comes in the contentment of being simply oneself, which cannot be found in the company of others.

Those of us for whom solitude is an acquired taste, those who fear it, must accept it on faith that we will be more whole, more spiritually centered than if we hadn't indulged it. The confirmation of that faith comes only after each experiment in solitude, however reluctantly undertaken. And for me it is not always successful. Sometimes there is too much baggage dragged along into solitude, too much anxiety, too many concerns, too much internal conflict. I have to give up and try again later.

Before I ever knew how far I had slipped into introversion, I began a prolonged search for a summer place that would get me away from the everyday hassles of living, committees, administrations, and students. It was a purely intuitive need—maybe *drive* is a better word—that I felt. I found it in Nova Scotia on a spot of land a mile off the highway, hidden behind a thick grove of trees, and on the Northumberland Strait. Here I knew I could restore my Self to its proper balance.

On our first drive from our home in Salt Lake City, we brought two of our sons along, sons whom we had not seen alone for any length of time since they married several years ago. The ride out with Ed and Charles was splendid. They spotted places in Nebraska and Iowa where they would like to own land. They walked around Boston and Cambridge with us for the first time in their lives and saw what we had been talking about all those years as we described the first five years of our marriage there. We went to a Boston Red Sox game and sat behind the catcher. Ed was so enthralled that he stood at the edge of the bleachers and stared onto Fenway Park as if it were a shrine. We left only when they turned off the lights.

The next day we drove the 600 miles to our home in Nova Scotia. We crossed the border from New Brunswick just as it was getting dark, and drove the last 150 miles scarcely seeing a light except from passing cars. Although there was a lot of banter and joking about the name of a town called Pugwash, the mood became increasingly sober. This clearly was a long way from civilization. I could feel my energy rising as we drew closer to my haven, but this was not the case for Ed, our most extroverted son. Sometime after Pugwash, when we had not seen a light for half an hour or more, I heard his voice coming from the backseat: "I wouldn't live here if you paid me a million dollars."

When we told them to start looking for a yellow mailbox on the left, the only marker of the driveway into our place, he said, "You mean you only know how to find this place by a mailbox?" There was real tension in his voice. We arrived at the house in pitch black. I dug out a flashlight and turned the lights on. After a preliminary search for dead mice, I called the three of them in. Ed looked as if he had just entered a Shanghai prison.

The next day, when Ed was clearly underwhelmed with this introvert's paradise, bordered on one side by a fir forest and on the other by water, we took them to New Glasgow, a town of nine thousand, where there was a Wal-Mart and a Wendy's. At the first sign of Wal-Mart, he hollered, "Yes, civilization." But he returned to normal only when he took his first bite of a Wendy's hamburger. "I'm home," he said. "I'm okay now."

I'm home too, Ed. Sunset is at low tide tonight. A few light clouds give texture to the sky, and the sun, turning to burnt umber, casts shades of pink, orange, blue, and purple on the drifting clouds. The water is low and still, revealing the ocean's bones. At low tide, once-submerged rock rears up to define coves that are secretly cloaked at high tide. Low tide reveals the ocean floor for what it is—the skeleton of the earth.

Tonight the water is still, glassy. The Spirit of God seems to hover over its face. A great blue heron wades just fifty feet away. He is at his best, his long legs moving ever so slowly, hesitating, one talon perched on a rock, then shifting to the other talon on another rock, never a slip, never a stumble. His talons have the span of an eagle's. He waits, calmly, waits, patiently, then plucks a small fish cleanly from the water, without even disturbing his reflection. I half expect him to look over and say, "Got one," but he keeps score only with his belly.

He doesn't think about beauty; he lives it. Humans live beauty at their own risk. Goethe's Faust faces damnation and survives only because he agrees not to cling too steadfastly to beauty. "In the moment that I say, 'Just linger a while, you are so beautiful,'" he tells his demon guide, "let that be my last day." Thomas Mann warns that beauty is a subject so dangerous, it should not be taught in the schools; its seductive power destroys us. His character Gustav von Aschenbach cleaves too long to beauty in Venice and dies of cholera, which he should have fled. Beauty is as dangerous as it is lovely.

Is the heron aware of this beautiful danger? I think not. It is his native home. It is not my native home. I have found my beauty on his turf, bought a cottage on the wooded and

beach-lined shore of the Northumberland Strait in Nova
Scotia, where I would gladly live out my days, clinging until I
rot. I spent part of the summer finishing a studio where
Louise can write, a little eight-by-ten-foot shed with shake
roof, shake shingles, hand-crafted doors and windows. A little
jewel, she calls it. We planted pole beans that wind their way
up long pine stakes connected by strings, and realized only
after a friend sent us a copy that we had followed William
Butler Yeats when he described his cottage at Innisfree:

> I will arise and go now, and go to Innisfree
> And a small cabin build there, of clay and wattles made;
> Nine bean-rows will I have there, a hive for the honey-bee,
> And live alone in the bee-loud glade.
> And I shall have some peace there, for peace comes drop-
> ping slow,
> Dropping from the veils of the morning to where the
> cricket sings;
> There midnight's all a-glimmer, and noon a purple glow,
> And evening full of the linnet's wings.
> I will arise and go now, for always night and day
> I hear lake water lapping with low sounds by the shore;
> While I stand on the roadway, or on the pavements gray,
> I hear it in the deep heart's core.

But soon, all too soon, I will leave my Innisfree, the
beans, tomatoes, and radishes mostly unpicked and uneaten,
the grapes rotting on the vines. I will leave the waters of
Northumberland lapping at the shore, sunsets that set the

world afire, the cawing crows, the silent heron, the place where I hear the deep heart's core. I will return to students filled with lust, passion, and naivete, brimming with the brashness of life, in which I too will join, sustained by the memory of beauty in my Innisfree. For solitude—and beauty—in proper doses, brings peace from God.

INTIMACY IS
WHAT YOU MAKE IT

$\mathcal{S}$ome folks in a position to know about the public discussions of intimacy tell me that the meaning of the word has narrowed. At least in contemporary American usage, it now refers almost exclusively to sexual relationships between partners. I hope I'm misquoting my sources on the subject, but I don't think so.

As dangerous as it is to take on all of American usage on any single word, especially a word as dear to the heart of younger people as *intimacy,* may I say, speaking strictly for myself, that it's nonsense to say that *intimacy* refers only to sexuality. It's the kind of definition that messes up the heads of couples as they grow older and engage less frequently for any number of reasons in sexual relationships. On any given day, going through the grocery line, I see magazine titles about sexual performance "at any age." "At any age" refers to any age up to the age of the editors, which may be forty, tops. Look at the pictures on the covers. Do those look like people "at any age"? I know that many older couples engage in sex. I know that many other older couples can't engage in sex because surgeons' scalpels have altered their bodies in hideous ways. Is that the end of intimacy?

What does it mean to be intimate with another person? After a dozen or so years of marriage, when sex has worked its way through the system, when sex is still good but not the be-all and end-all of a relationship, when sex leaves you longing for something deeper, something richer, people begin asking what it means to be intimate. That's the question a friend put to me a few months ago in an unexpected e-mail. "My new focus is intimacy," she said. "Do you have anything to say about intimacy?"

I wrote back that I had said all that I had to say on the subject in *Eating Chocolates and Dancing in the Kitchen*.

She didn't buy that. "So, you said *all* you have to say about intimacy in marriage in the *Chocolates* book? I find it hard to believe you *ever* say *all* you have to say. Maybe it's just me. How about you, Louise? I bet you have a few words to say about intimacy in marriage."

Louise was more cautious. She asked for clarification: "So, what exactly do you want to know about intimacy in marriage? I want specific questions here."

Our friend replied that all around her were "unfulfilling, unhappy, combative, tolerated" marriages. After more than a dozen years of marriage, she and her husband were looking for "real intimacy in all areas—emotional, physical, spiritual." Her questions were searching and thought-provoking: "Have you grown naturally together or have you had to set goals and work toward intimacy? At what stage in your relationship have you enjoyed the greatest amount of true intimacy? Is it something you have to continue to work toward? How do you do it? How would you define intimacy in marriage? There are your questions."

At this point, I was happy to let Louise pick up the correspondence. She wrote back: "A question like what is intimacy in marriage seems like a hefty subject to take on. So I'll say this—it's not like the movies. You have to keep working at it. Life gets in the way. It's easy just to think you're too busy to have an intimate relationship with your husband, but in fact, it's fairly critical. So you go away for weekends and you talk whenever you can get it in.

"Tom likes to talk, and he's a pretty good listener if you repeat it often enough. We just keep working at it. It never gets easy. Marriage and family is never easy. Even when it's good, it's not easy. Don't let those comic essays of Tom's make you fret. They're all true. But you're absolutely right—he doesn't write about the really hard stuff. Who would be able to stand it? And, of course, even the hard stuff is funny from a distance. But we still plug through all the same issues: money, children, sex, God, and now we talk about retirement (which I don't see happening in any near future). And then there's this: after you've been married for a really long time, you've heard every story a billion times, and so has he, so how do you keep it all fresh? Beats me. Do you have any answers? Love, Louise."

The more I think about it, the more I think intimacy is

elusive because it's a shared state of mind. Intimacy can never be one-sided. Nor can it be precisely defined. You can't take an intimacy test and find that your Intimacy Quotient is a seven on a scale of ten, although I'm sure such tests exist. Maybe that's why so many people wonder whether their relationship is intimate. They can't measure it exactly, and it can't be compared to someone else's to get a clear measure. Still, I think there are some things that intimacy is and is not. It is certainly not selfishness, neglect, or abuse. Intimacy cannot exist in a hostile or unfriendly environment. It just isn't going to happen.

Intimacy is a mutual sense that God, however near at times, however distant at others, is watching over you and sanctions your relationship. You are his children, and even in the worst of times, he blesses your union. Even in the worst of times, small miracles happen.

Intimacy is a willingness to share doubts.

Intimacy is a mutual trust that you are faithful to each other and that you act in behalf of each other's best interest.

Intimacy is a willingness to let go, to allow the other person time alone, time for solitude, time for other friends, even when it's hard.

Intimacy is taking pleasure in being together with friends.

Intimacy is taking pleasure in being alone with each other.

Intimacy is a quiet touch, a bump of the knees, a brush of the hands.

Intimacy is touching—any time, any place.

INTIMACY IS WHAT YOU MAKE IT

Intimacy is going for a ride in the car or a walk in the park.

Intimacy is being spontaneous.

Intimacy is being comfortable across the room from each other.

Intimacy is a hug and a good long kiss.

Intimacy is spoon hugging that does not lead to sex.

Intimacy is spoon hugging that leads to sex.

Intimacy is being comfortable without hugging and kissing while sharing personal thoughts and attitudes.

Intimacy is going to a movie the other person really wants to see.

Intimacy is a willingness to let the other person stay up late when you are tired.

Intimacy is a willingness to talk at any time of day or night.

Intimacy is a good conversation about almost anything.

Intimacy is understanding each other without saying a word.

Intimacy is saying what's on your mind.

Intimacy is teaming up to do things together.

Intimacy is doing things alone to rediscover yourself.

Intimacy is playfulness with each other.

Intimacy is having a sense of humor about your foibles.

Intimacy is a good belly laugh together.

Intimacy is crying together.

Intimacy is reading together.

Intimacy is praying together.

Intimacy is sharing your deepest feelings, your greatest joy, your deepest sorrow, knowing that your partner will understand and not betray you.

Intimacy is a cup of hot chocolate together in bed— morning, noon, or night.

Here is one example of an "intimate" scene:

A fire is blazing in the cobblestone fireplace; a little cover of clouds hints of rain; the languid sea, moving toward high tide, laps gently on the shore. We are alone, Louise and I. The guests have gone home, and now remains for me the one true love I have ever had in my life, the only girl I ever kissed with such passion that I couldn't find her lips on the first try. Maybe because she was the only girl I ever really kissed and I hadn't yet learned how to locate lips. We are here together.

Louise is sitting twelve feet away, playing solitaire on her computer; I am sitting on the sofa with my laptop, writing. It's our new intimacy. Younger people would scoff. "That's not intimacy. That's distance." But they're wrong. It's intimacy. Occasionally one of us breaks the silence with a comment.

"I think I'll write Erica a letter. What are you writing?"

"I'm playing backgammon online."

We are comfortable with each other. I put down my game, walk past Louise, and give her a kiss on the top of her head. "I love you," I say. "You're beautiful." She snorts just a bit. I know what she's thinking. She's thinking that I haven't any judgment at all when it comes to her, that I'm visually disabled, that I'm lying my face off, as she's fond of saying.

The fire is crackling. I think how much I relish Louise's

energy, her perfectly timed wit, those gorgeous lips, her sexy alto voice belting out Gershwin and Porter songs, a voice that seduced me thirty-eight years ago. More than likely, when she's finished her solitaire and I've finished my backgammon, we'll sit down and stare at the fire and ruminate. Maybe we'll talk about the bite she has on her head from a little black fly that's particularly nasty in these parts in May. Maybe we'll talk about my aching back. More likely, we'll sit and snuggle—or not—put on a movie we've seen a dozen times, and enjoy being together.

Soon she says, "Do you miss me?"

"Well, I can enjoy you from here if I have to," I say. "Maybe you should get online and we'll play against each other."

We could, of course, just get out the backgammon board and play at the table. But this is a new idea. Louise gets online. We meet. We play two games. Louise wins both of them. She got lucky. I quit. She says I'm a sore loser.

"I still love you," I say.

Defining intimacy is like handling a delicate flower. Not too much mauling, not too much clinging. It's best with a little play and humor, and all in small doses. Intimacy is something we work at every day, though not with a game plan or a calendar in front of us. Every day presents new possibilities for tension, disagreement, discussion, sadness. Every day is a new search for intimacy in its ever-changing forms. Some days we win. Some days we lose. Some days we feel so fragile that we could break apart. But we never give up on intimacy. If we ignored it, it would drift away like a blossom on a stream.

STOP THE CLOCK

I've quit wearing my watch or looking at a calendar unless I absolutely have to. The clock, I've realized, is a tyrant. From the sound of the alarm rousting me from calm sleep to the five-minute shower, to the four-and-a-half-minute poached egg, to the thirty-minute walk, to the fifty-five-minute commute, to the hour-and-fifteen-minute classes, to the dinner hour, to the 9:00 P.M. *Law and Order* on television interspersed with eight three-minute commercial breaks, my life is not fully my own. Convention, temperature, health scientists, marketers, and clocks have taken me hostage.

Even the shape of my fleeting time has been decided by others. When digital clocks came on the market, my sons wanted one. It was the easy way to tell time, and a sad day for them when their teacher said they had to learn how to tell time on an analog clock. I read an article back then by some smart person who pointed out that digital clocks have reconfigured the way we experience time. With analog clocks, time flows, if only in circles. At least with the movement of the

138

hands, we have a sense of continuity. With digital clocks, time becomes fragmentary—one second, then another second, then another second.

Either way—analog or digital—time conforms to nothing natural, neither to the natural rhythms of sunrise and sunset nor to the rhythms of the heartbeat, nor to the rising and falling tide, nor to the phases of the moon. There are still people who live their lives according to natural time, people we consider "primitive." They rise with the sun and go to bed with the moon; they live by the seasons but are unaware of the days of the week or the hour of the day. These "primitives" never say, Is it time for lunch yet? Is it time for *Law and Order?* Is it time for bed? They never ask how many hours a night they should sleep. They never keep a record of how long they live. They never compare the time on the radio with their own time and become anxious because their watch is slow.

Clocks are harbingers of anxiety, of miles per hour, of early death by speed. As if a regular watch weren't bad enough, some obsessive actuary has developed a watch that can tell us our life expectancy at a glance. We program information into the little wizard, and it reports what we hardly want to know—how many years, months, weeks, days, minutes, and seconds we have to live if we are "average." I have wondered what happens to people wearing a watch like that when they zero out. Do they gather the family around and drop dead? If they survive zero, do they start talking about how they are now "living on borrowed time"? What if they die prematurely? In my mind is an obituary that reads, "Fred Punter died this morning, six years, three weeks, two days, four hours, twenty-three minutes, and six seconds short of the expected time on his actuarial watch. We're so sorry, Fred. We were all cheering for you. We thought you could make it, but you punted on third down."

I know someone has to keep track of time; someone has to regulate it. Before time zones were created and time standardized, cross-country trains collided because nobody had standardized time zones. Maybe those collisions gave rise to the story problems in math that are the bane of every grade-school student: "If a train leaves New York at an average speed of 75 miles per hour, and a train leaves Los Angeles one hour and 23 minutes later at a speed of 57.8993 miles per hour . . ." I know that the order of the world demands timekeepers.

When my mind is up to no good, I wonder if there is such a thing as time if nobody is there to tell the time. I wonder, as some philosophers have, if time ever repeats itself in a pattern of eternal recurrence? Will I be sitting on this spot, writing these words on this laptop at some future time, exactly as I am doing now? Will Louise be sitting beside me reading the same biography of Edna St. Vincent Millay? If time is relative, as Einstein has shown with $E=MC^2$, will travelers to outer space return to find their spouses have died of old age while they are still young? Is there someplace where time stands still? Is there absolutely no place you can go to escape time?

How would our lives be different if we never calculated

life expectancy? If we never kept track of age? We wouldn't know whether Mary had lived longer than Myrtle or Myrtle longer than Mary. We wouldn't have to report our age in the obituaries, because we wouldn't know our age. Would it matter? Would we put hundreds of thousands of actuaries out of work because they wouldn't know how to calculate insurance premiums? Would we focus less on longevity and more on the quality of the lives we live? Would we need to set "goals" so we can lead busy and productive lives, joining the ranks of "highly successful" people?

I saw a television special recently about a guy who was determined to live to be 125. He monitored every bite of food he ate. He measured his blood sugar five times a day. He exercised constantly. He went to dances for teenagers to keep himself moving and tried to look joyous as his aging body failed to keep up with theirs. He was in his sixties. Staying alive until 125 was the sole focus of his life. "I figure if I can make it to 80, then someone will have a cure for cancer," he said. "Then I can make it to 100, because my heart will be strong from good food and exercise. Then someone will have a cure for heart disease." Watch out for Parkinson's disease, sir.

To see him is to know that he has no life. What is 125 but an indicator of how little living he really did? Is there a difference between the length of time lived and the quality of living done? Did Mozart live more in his 36 years than this guy in his 125? What guarantees us that time measures truth? We exercise exactly 45 minutes a day, no less, because if it's less, if we cover just 2.99999 miles instead of 3.0000001 miles, the body is going to notice and not respond to the exercise we put in. The body is a carefully calibrated machine, we hear, and it knows, it knows just what the clock knows. Sometimes I walk for just 29 minutes to see if I'll drop dead for not walking 30.

People who live strictly by the clock, writes Alan Lightman, "think their bodies don't exist. They live by mechanical time. They rise at seven o'clock in the morning. They eat their lunch at noon and their supper at six. They arrive at their appointments on time, precisely by the clock. . . . They work forty hours a week, read the Sunday paper on Sunday, play chess on Tuesday nights. When their stomach growls, they look at their watch to see if it is time to eat" (*Einstein's Dreams* [New York: Pantheon Books, 1993], 25).

I keep vigil for opportunities to shed my watch. I go to the woods and listen to the birds. I sit by the ocean and watch the surf. I sit by a stream and listen to the flowing water. I take off my watch. I leave it home. It takes a lot of restraint to leave my watch home on the dresser. I can hear it calling to me as I drive away. Tommmmmm. . . . . . . youuuuuuuu . . . . . . neeeeeeeed. . . . . . . .meeeeeeee. It's prison, slavery, confinement, anxiety calling.

When I'm not wearing my watch, I write until I'm done. I read until I've finished. I garden until I'm tired. I sleep until I wake up. I wear my jammies all day without showering or dressing. I listen to the rhythms of the earth, put myself in harmony with its natural ebbs and flows, absorb its pulsations. I listen more carefully to my inner voice, which I can now hear because I'm not worried about "the time," and I never ever ask that inner voice, "What time is it? How much time do I have?"

Outside the window is the rolling surf of a November ocean. A brisk wind and bright sun create ever-changing moods. Sometime soon, maybe later today or tomorrow, I'll get some packing boxes and begin the work I came to do. But for this moment, God's world spreads out before me—God's grandeur, for this moment, is my grandeur. In this moment, time stands still. This moment is everything. It is all I have.

THEY'RE MY GIFTS,
I'M AFRAID

One day a student, whom I'll call Benjamin, came to my office to ask for a letter of recommendation so he could go to law school. Our paths had first crossed when I was teaching an intermediate German class, in which Benjamin enrolled straight out of high school.

Midway through the semester I had the students make oral presentations to the class in German. For some, this was torture. They stood in front of the class, clasping and wringing their hands, rolling their eyes toward the ceiling, and shifting from foot to foot. They stumbled on words they knew and uttered German with unrecognizable pronunciation. They hated the humiliation of speaking German in front of their friends, and they would stand in front of the group, twist their lips into curls, fiddle with their hair, and say, "Gee, I hate this."

Benjamin felt none of this timidity. He asked in front of several students after class one day if he could sing his assignment. I said, "Yes. Absolutely." A little madness makes a class more interesting.

On the appointed day, Benjamin stood before the class and announced that he would sing a solo from Mozart's *Zauberflöte.*

I braced myself. Was he really going to murder Mozart? I tried to think of what a first-year college student could sing from the *Zauberflöte,* certainly Mozart's most fanciful and possibly most trying operatic gem. It was no joke. I no longer remember what he sang, but I do remember being stunned that this adolescent stood before the class with the poise of a trained performer and sang an aria from a Mozart opera. The class burst into wild applause as he finished.

After taking a two-year leave from the university to do missionary work, Benjamin returned to pursue a major in vocal performance. He sang the role of Sarastro in a university production of the *Zauberflöte,* a bass part with a stunning aria. Benjamin was a star.

This, then, was the Benjamin who came to my office door that day. I repeated his request in my mind: Would I write a letter of recommendation in support of his application to law school?

"I'm sorry, Benjamin," I said, "I won't write you a letter for law school."

Benjamin looked mystified. "You won't write me a letter?"

"Nope," I said. "Not for law school."

"How come?"

"Because you have no business going to law school. You're

a singer. A really good singer. You could be singing opera. Why do you want to go to law school?"

"Well, I thought it was a good way to make a living."

"For the right people," I said. "But you're not a lawyer, you're an artist. Do you know what lawyers do? Do you even know a lawyer?"

"No."

"Do you know Professor Rogers in the School of Music?"

"Yeah. The singer."

"Right. Did you know he got a law degree from Harvard and, when he realized he'd made a mistake, he turned around and got a doctorate in vocal performance, which was his first love?"

"No."

"Do you know what will happen to you if you go to law school? You'll still become a singer. Only you'll be several years late and a whole lot more broke getting under way. I won't write you a letter for law school. If you want me to support an application for graduate study in vocal performance, come back."

Benjamin came back. I wrote him a letter.

Speaking from experience, I can say that it is no easy matter to embrace our own gifts and abilities and to have the courage to exercise them. Sometimes it means becoming a doctor in a family of artists; a longshoreman in a family of lawyers; a grasshopper in a family of ants. It may take frank and painful discussion with those who love us most to say that our gifts lie on different grounds than theirs and that we must pursue them. Sometimes this comes in advanced years, when the ghosts of parents long dead still seem to be whispering rules in our ears.

Occasionally the very people who are trained to help us find our gifts err in an unsuspecting moment. When our son Sam returned from his mission and began his university studies again, he was confused about what course to pursue. The mission had given him much to think about; he had discovered things about himself he didn't know, and he had no vision of his future. This is not uncommon for students, and universities have counseling centers designed to help. Louise and I suggested that he take some aptitude and personality tests that might help him understand more about himself and what fields of interest might inspire him. He took the test and scored high in two areas: social services and fashion. Quite different, one might even think incompatible, interests.

The adviser was thrown off as well, and in an unguarded moment said of the fashion scores, "Well, Sam, I see you're getting in touch with your femmy side."

Whatever else he might have said that day was of no relevance whatsoever. Sam came home thinking he had no legitimacy as a male, and by the time he talked to us, he was overwrought. *How can it be,* he was asking himself, *that there's no place for me if I'm so interested in fashion?*

It is true. Sam is interested in fashion. He has been design conscious since he was young, although Louise and I had never paid much attention to it. He's meticulous about his own clothing, deigns now to tell me or Louise when we're wearing the wrong thing, and tracks all of the major designers.

I began wondering how I could help him legitimize this very genuine interest, and almost immediately I had a solution. Steven, a good friend of ours, manages one of the premiere jewelry stores in the area. It's a store that caters to the crème de la crème of society and sells jewelry and china as works of art. Moreover, Steven, himself a man of fine taste, has been an athlete—football, basketball, and baseball—and a student-body president who knew everyone's name in a school of two thousand students. I called Steven, explained the situation, and asked if he would meet Sam, show him around the store, and help him feel more comfortable with his own personal makeup.

Steven was more than accommodating. Sam went dressed in a suit, white shirt, and tie, the norm for that store. Steven met him at the door, introduced him to the staff as "my friend Sam," and explained to him that men who have the means collect fine Swiss watches with exquisite mechanisms. Watch collecting is a man's hobby in fine jewelry, he said, as he pulled a $25,000 watch out of the display case and explained its workings. Then they went into the basement of the building, where a staff of artisans were making fine jewelry. Steven introduced Sam around and let him observe jewelry being made.

By the time Sam got home, he was comfortable with himself, with his natural interests, and with being a little different from others. In the meantime, he has picked up the other side of his interests, social services, and works in a home for victims of cerebral palsy.

The problem is that our biases, the ways in which we stereotype how people should be, turn some of the most gifted members of our society into outsiders. I could be much more self-righteous about how I've handled these matters if I didn't have to confess to fathering Ed. My son Ed, like Sam, is a very different animal from me. But Ed, unfortunately, is nine years older than Sam, and I wasn't as astute about supporting personal differences when he was growing up. Ed loved to sleep in, play video games, and avoid school work. I, on the other hand, rise early, read or write, and do course preparations. This led to serious conflicts during Ed's teen years. There were times when I could not get Ed up for school. I'd go to his room, shake him, slam drawers and doors, and, as a last resort, yank his mattress out from under him. I'd push him out to catch the bus, and after he had missed it and I had driven him to school for the zillionth time, I laid down the law. "If you miss the bus again," I said, "you're walking to school." That was five miles.

Within twenty-four hours, he missed the bus. It was Minnesota. It was winter. The temperature was hovering around or below zero. I booted him out, under protest from both Ed and Louise. "He has to learn some discipline," I told her. "I don't see how he's going to survive in the world." The first day Ed had to make his way to school, he flagged a taxi. The ride would cost him ten dollars, the driver said. Ed had two dollars. He walked. To my knowledge, he never did have enough to take a cab.

For years I despaired about Ed. I saw no place for him in human civilization. He continued to ace video games, do poorly in school, and sleep in on Saturdays. When it came time for high school graduation, I went over his course credits with him. He was two credits short. I went ballistic. I had enrolled him in a correspondence course to make up for a failed biology class. "When were you planning to do this?" I hollered.

"Thursday," he said.

"Graduation is Friday," I yelled. "You have to be done before Thursday or you won't graduate. Where is your textbook?"

"I don't know." He shrugged his shoulders and looked at me with complete indifference.

I went rummaging through the house, through Ed's room, through his brothers' rooms, through my study, through Louise's study. No textbook. I went to the garage. There, in a stack of old newspapers, was the book. I pulled Ed out of school for the entire last week, collected his lessons as he completed them, delivered them to the continuing education office, and got his grade reported to the high school. He graduated with no more than fifteen minutes to spare on his deadline.

That was Ed—past tense. That was me—past tense, I hope. Ed is now an operations manager at a Fortune 500 company. He uses computer programs that I cannot fathom—possibly the spinoff from video games; he manages a team of people; he teaches a Sunday School class with humor, insight, and aplomb. I have apologized to Ed dozens of times for my crude fathering. This essay is one last apology.

What happened? In spite of my torpedoes, in spite of the fact that I wasn't looking for Ed's gifts, he found them and went with them. One day while he was working on a computer program, I asked him about a statistics course he was taking. "I hear statistics is really a miserable subject," I said.

"Not really," he said. "It's fun."

I have realized, all too slowly, that Ed and I are different. He is extroverted. I am introverted. He works statistically. I work intuitively. He does things he really wants to do. I do things I don't want to do, because I'm "disciplined"—sometimes a disadvantage to authentic living, I now realize. If I hadn't been so busy disciplining myself and Ed, I might have seen that I could learn something from him, something about doing things, something about being in the world. Yes. Something about *being* in the world. Recently he set up a computer program for me to track my budget. "Does anyone know how to do this better than you?" Louise asked him.

"Nope," he said. "I'm the best." He was not being arrogant.

For others, the cost of overly strict rules and abusive upbringing is much higher. A man was recently honored for being the oldest student in Great Britain. He was 107. The photo in the London *Times* showed him looking brightly into the camera. Fred Moore showed no sign at all that he was a day over eighty. His neatly combed white hair, finely chiseled features, and broad smile said this was a man who was aged but not old. He told the correspondent that he didn't enjoy his early schooldays and that he was making up for lost time. His teachers in the 1890s tied his arm behind his back to "cure" his left-handedness. "I was left-handed, but they forced me to write with my right hand," he said. "It upset me and made me nervous. I used to think all the other boys in my class were better than me." Discouraged that he could not fit in, Fred dropped out of school. When he retired at age sixty-five, he began taking weekly painting classes. "I go to class every Tuesday . . . I wouldn't give it up for anything. I don't think about my age. I just enjoy producing art," he said. The article doesn't say whether he paints with his right or left hand, but maybe that's too obvious.

Sometimes society has created hurdles to prevent us from discovering and becoming ourselves. For centuries, women were considered ill suited for education. Consider these quotes from distinguished Germans of past centuries on the education of women:

Martin Luther (b. 1483)
No cloak or dress looks worse on a woman than when she pretends to be intelligent.

Women should not be praised for being eloquent. It appears better when they stammer and cannot speak well. That seems them much better.

Men have a broad chest and narrow hips. Therefore they have more understanding than women, who have narrow breasts and wide hips and buttocks so that they can stay at home, sit in the house, clean, and bear and raise children.

Women lack strength of body and understanding.

Ulrich von Hutten (b. 1488)

Intelligence? As if there were women who loved it. They like a pretty figure and wealth.

Justus M. Iser (b. 1720)

Concerning maidens, oh, I wouldn't want to marry one that can read and write.

Immanuel Kant (b. 1724)

Learned women need their books and their watch just to carry them around, so that they are seen. Their watches are generally stopped or not set properly.

Becoming a whole person means first knowing that these impositions of the rules and ideas of others, though sometimes created with the best of intentions, may be fully wrong, and we must ignore them if we are to become fully the children God created us to be.

Unlike plants, where onions come from onions, radishes from radishes, and tulips from tulips, members of a family all have different personalities, different gifts, different abilities. It's like a family of onions suddenly producing a petunia. Remember the old song, "I'm a Lonely Little Petunia in an Onion Patch"? Humans are like that.

It's impossible for a petunia to get instructions from an onion about how to develop its talents. The onion doesn't have a clue. It may be a gifted onion, but it's a lousy petunia. If I am a natural mathematician in a family of artists who can barely multiply two and two, I can't get any help from them about how I should develop. I will have to find other math whizzes.

One thing I know for sure is that our gifts are to be used in behalf of ourselves and others. They are our gifts to bless the world. We can't use them if we don't know what they are, or if we have buried them as the poor man buried his single talent in Jesus' parable. Accepting our gifts feels risky. It is risky. Sometimes it means falling flat on your face, getting up, dusting yourself off, and going at it again while those around you are clucking their tongues and saying, "I told you so." Sometimes it means pursuing your gifts with spouse and children on your back. It doesn't much matter whether you are in your twenties, as Benjamin was, or in your sixties, as I am. The question that every person has to answer, over and over, is, "Am I going to take this risk to become more of what God made me to be, or am I going to plateau out?"

"Self-trust," Emerson once wrote, "is the essence of hero-ism."

Not so long ago the most famous of all American pianists,

Van Cliburn, made a memorable return to the concert stage. The year was 1994, and Mr. Cliburn had not had a serious concert tour since 1978, sixteen years earlier. Rumors floated through the press—rumors that he had a weak memory and therefore a small repertoire, that he was suffering from depression and anxiety. The press knows how to make anyone and everyone look like a twinkie.

Cliburn's fame as a pianist came early. I suspect every American who is old enough will recall front-page newspaper photographs in 1958 of that most dreaded of Russian premiers, Nikita Khrushchev, the man who took off his shoe and pounded the podium in the United Nations, the man who threatened to "bury" the West—we all assumed he meant with nuclear weapons—giving Cliburn a big Russian bear hug for winning the gold medal at the first Tchaikovsky piano competition in Moscow. He had done this by beating a horde of Russian pianists at their own game, playing Tchaikovsky's *Piano Concerto No. 1 in B-flat.* It was a stunning accomplishment in the darkest hours of the Cold War. Cliburn's gangly figure, boyish demeanor, and virtuosity captured the imagination of people the world over, not the least of them being hero-hungry Americans. He toured the country, playing the beloved Tchaikovsky concerto to packed houses.

But now Cliburn was making a comeback on the occasion of his sixtieth birthday. After a preliminary concert in San Diego, he made his grand entrance in the Hollywood Bowl in the company of a Russian orchestra. The program included Cliburn's own piano transcription of "The

Star-Spangled Banner," Aaron Copland's *Lincoln Portrait*, with Cliburn himself as pianist and narrator, and two mega-piano concertos: Tchaikovsky's *Piano Concerto No. 1 in B-flat* and Rachmaninoff's daunting *Piano Concerto No. 3*.

Of course the ever-hungry-for-blood American press was waiting for Cliburn to fall flat, and he did not disappoint them. After the first half of the program, in which critics noted a few bobbles, came intermission. Remaining for the second half was the Mount Everest, the Rachmaninoff concerto. Intermission lasted and lasted and lasted, according to one report, for an hour or more. The Russian orchestra came out on stage and sat around, then milled around. The crowd of 14,035 became restless and resorted to rhythmic clapping. Someone was seen rushing a stack of music backstage. Then a loudspeaker voice announced that Mr. Cliburn was feeling a bit dizzy but would soon return. All of this led to speculation by critics that Mr. Cliburn had suffered something like a panic attack after the not-too-great first half of the evening and was hiding out in his dressing room. "Did he drive off in his Bronco?" one wondered.

Finally Mr. Cliburn returned to the stage and announced that he would not be playing the Rachmaninoff concerto after all. He proceeded to play a few encore pieces while the Russian orchestra sat on stage doing nothing except, possibly, daydreaming of basking on Laguna Beach. Many in the audience demanded a refund, which promoters refused because the concert had gone on after intermission, even though only music buffs knew what Cliburn had played, since he didn't announce the four pieces he performed. Happy birthday, Van, and welcome back to the world of public humiliation.

I suspect everyone who has ever gone through the agony of a music recital must feel some empathy with Van Cliburn. I know I do. During the winter of 1954 my piano teacher, Mrs. Johnson, told me that she would like me to begin preparing for a solo recital. It would take about a year to prepare, she said. Although, at age thirteen, I had risen to become the best of her students, I lacked technical competence. When I skipped practicing scales and the Hanon exercises, Mrs. Johnson never reprimanded me. "Practice these for next week," she would say. I never did.

As the year progressed, I began to worry that I was not ready. I was making mistakes. I was muddling runs. I was forgetting passages. Some days were not too bad; others were hideous. I never could play consistently. I was not ready. A solo recital in the presence of friends and relatives was a big deal. I felt vulnerable, as vulnerable as any adolescent is capable of feeling.

Ready or not, Sunday, March 13, 1954, arrived, dangerously close to the Ides of March. I had become increasingly shaky. Though I had learned and memorized six serious pieces, all the notes seemed to be running together in a massive brain meltdown. During practice the day before the recital, passages where I had never faltered began to wobble. Family came. Neighbors came. My friends came. Barry the Bully sat on the front row. My mother said I had to invite him. "What will he think when he sees everyone else on the block coming to the house and he's not been invited?"

Now Barry sat in my living room. If I screwed up, he would be delirious. I was sure of it. A recital in the presence of mine enemies. Was that worse than a recital in the presence of those who loved me? Grandma Swindle was there. Grandma loved me. When I practiced, she would sit at the piano and rest her quavering arm on the wood curvature at the end of the keyboard. After I had practiced my recital pieces, she would say, "Now play 'O My Father.'" And while I played a schlocky rendition of the hymn, she listened with deep fervor, eyes partly shut, worshipping. She loved me. For her I could do no wrong.

As I sat there awaiting the signal, "Dead man playing," our living room packed, I realized I could not remember how the first piece started. It was a condensed and simplified version of Grieg's *Piano Concerto in C# Minor,* the one everyone recognizes from *Song of Norway.* It was to be the no-brainer, warm-up piece, the one to give me confidence to sail through the rest of the recital. Was the high chord two or was it three octaves above middle C? I had to start on the right octave because the opening of the piece chorded from the treble to the bass clef—BOOM—TA DA BOOM—TA DA BOOM—TA DA BOOM—TA DA BOOM. If I started too high, it would sound like the "Dance of the Sugar-Plum Fairy." What if I started too low? I didn't know. I tried to tap it out. I tried to imagine starting at the end and going backwards. I was too nervous. I couldn't be sure.

THEY'RE MY GIFTS, I'M AFRAID

The pile of music I was playing lay just ten feet away beside the piano, the Grieg concerto on top. But I felt too self-conscious to walk over and look at it. We were almost ready to start, and it was uncool to peek. Someone might notice. Someone like Barry. He would know for sure I was about to choke. He'd love it. I couldn't give him the satisfaction.

Mrs. Johnson, my piano teacher of six years, was now standing before the gathering. She was a homely woman. I was all the more aware of it at that moment. Her hook nose, squat body, buck teeth, and facial hair were more than my adolescent shame could endure. How could I be aligned with such an ugly woman? I was embarrassed. I was ashamed to be embarrassed. And I couldn't remember where the concerto started.

"I've never had a student this age who could play as beautifully as Tommy Plummer," she was saying.

Tom. Not Tommy. I used to be Tommy. Not Tommy now. I'm Tom.

My palms were already sweating, my fingers shaking. I had never once played even in a group recital with calm hands. How was I going to survive the next hour of a solo recital? Mrs. Johnson had finished her introduction. Friends, neighbors, and enemies all applauded. It was time for the Grieg.

I stepped to the bench, sat, and stared at the keys. Where did it start? There? No, that's too high. There. That's it. And my hands came down solidly. Unretractably. An octave low. I remember a chill freezing my brain. Mrs. Johnson had assured me on more than one occasion that I knew how to get out of mistakes better than any of her students. Now was the time. Onward. And I played onward. Why didn't I make a little joke and start over? "Just kidding." "Just seeing if you're there." "Hi ya, Barry." Because I was fourteen, and I was taking the biggest risk of my young life. Down the scale we went. BOOM—TA DA BOOM—TA DA BOOM—TA DA BOOM—TA DA BOOM. Only without that last TA DA BOOM, because I was at the bottom of the piano and out of keys—not more than ten seconds into the recital, and I was out of keys.

It didn't all go so badly after that. The Beethoven, the Debussy, the DeFalla. It just felt bad. After that tortured hour, kindly neighbors and friendly family applauded wildly. To put an end to the humiliation, I raised both hands in the style of President Eisenhower, a gesture that I immediately regretted. Everyone laughed. And thus ended the worst hour of my young life.

"I'm quitting Mrs. Johnson," I told my parents the next morning.

"Then you call her and tell her you're quitting," my mother said.

I went straight to the phone. "Mrs. Johnson? This is Tom Plummer. Fine, thanks. I'm calling to say that I'm quitting piano lessons." I heard an audible grunt from her end. She said something about doing what I needed to do, and we hung up. I never saw her or talked to her again, which I now regret.

The next month I started lessons with another teacher, a rigorous technician in her late seventies. Her purple-tinted hair camouflaged a tough woman, whose claim to fame was having trained concert pianists. On the first lesson she told me my posture needed correction. She started me on a daily program of major and minor scales in all keys and J. S. Bach's "Two-Part Inventions." I practiced them all. For dessert I was to learn Mozart's first piano sonata. I fell somewhere into the lower third of her students. Over the next five years, she never discussed a solo recital with me.

I am still connected to music, but in a way that is more realistic. I'm a ward organist. Soon I'll be starting organ lessons to improve my skills, to make better use of the organ's capacities, to get confidence in using the pedals. A thousand times every Sunday, Louise assures me it's a good thing. "I love it when you play the organ," she says again and again. "I just love it." She sits by the organ in the choir seats so we can be together during meetings. She loves me when I play the organ. My wife loves me when I use one of my gifts. But I'll never ever play an organ recital.

I work on other gifts, hoping that in some small way they will make a difference, that I will contribute in my own way to life on earth. I have no delusions of grandeur as I once had. I just want to make some difference—maybe just for a moment or two to someone. I take great comfort in the

words of Paul when he described the community of Christ in
1 Corinthians 12:

> A body is not one single organ, but many.
> Suppose the foot should say, "Because I am not
> a hand, I do not belong to the body," it does
> belong to the body none the less. Suppose the
> the ear were to say, "Because I am not an eye, I
> do not belong to the body," it does still belong
> to the body. If the body were all eye, how could
> it hear? If the body were all ear, how could it
> smell? But, in fact, God appointed each limb
> and organ to its own place in the body, as he
> chose. If the whole were one single organ, there
> would not be a body at all; in fact, however,
> there are many different organs, but one body.
> The eye cannot say to the hand, "I do not need
> you"; nor the head to the feet, "I do not need
> you." Quite the contrary: those organs of the
> body which seem to be more frail than others
> are indispensable, and those parts of the body
> which we regard as less honorable are treated
> with special honour. (*New English Bible,* 1
> Corinthians 12:12–20)

Sometimes I would rather be the brain than the pinky.
Or, especially as it becomes more difficult to climb out of my
car, I'd like to be the backbone. Paul assures me that I'm all

right. I don't need to look for more glamorous jobs if I'm exercising the gifts God gave me. There's no need to covet, no need to be critical of someone else. My first job is to put the gifts I have to work, knowing that they have a place in the world. My second job is to work on gifts that are still in stages of latent or early development. My third job is to remember what my gifts are and extend them.

The Peter Principle describes the inclination in institutions to promote people to the level of their incompetence. The best barber I've ever had has been made the manager of his own shop and two affiliated shops, with half a dozen permanent barbers and a couple of dozen part-time barbers. He's having a hard time of it. Haircutting is the job he does best. Management is wearing him out. He refuses to give up haircutting because he loves it, but his days have become fourteen to sixteen hours as he tries to cover both jobs.

Sometimes even being the pinky feels risky. Even pinkies get sprained. That's the risk of knowing and exercising one's gifts. Doing the right thing is no guarantee that you won't fall into a rosebush once in a while. "Seek ye earnestly the best gifts, always remembering for what they are given; for verily I say unto you, they are given for the benefit of those who love me and keep all my commandments . . . that all may be benefited that seek or that ask of me. . . . For there are many gifts, and to every man is given a gift by the Spirit of God" (D&C 46:8–11).

THE HEARTS
OF THE FATHERS

My father would be 103 years old now if he hadn't died at age 65. I've been thinking more and more about him. The young man in my head says I should be forgetting him now. He's been dead so long. The old man in my head says I should embrace him. He's become omnipresent. When I speak of education, his voice becomes mine. When I go to the theater, I'm on his turf. When I pass the public library, he talks to me: it's the people's university. After all these years he has become more powerful, not less. I used to think I should escape my father. It's a bad idea. Now I want to embrace him.

Just as he used to embrace me. He snuggled me to him in the mornings when, as a small boy, I climbed into bed with him and Mother. It was one of the best times of childhood. Lying on his side, he would wrap his arm around my chest, hold me tightly, and fall asleep. The sweet odor of his body signaled safety, peace, and security.

In my twenties, when I was in college, I was preparing for my first final exam in a German literature course. Volumes of names, dates, and titles piled up on my desk, ideas that had no hook in my memory. I would fail this exam, I thought. As the night wore on, everything seemed to slip from my head onto the floor. I lay down for a short nap, but my body stiffened like a piece of Formica.

I remembered then my father's hugs. I went to his room and woke him. "Dad," I said, "I'm a nervous wreck. Could you hug me like you used to?"

He pulled me to him and wrapped his arm around my chest. He still smelled the same. The peace and security of a time long gone came over me. I fell asleep for a little while, a grown man wrapped in my father's arm. When I awoke, I finished my studies and wrote the exam.

I think about my father. I think about Malachi's words—the hearts of the fathers, the hearts of the children. I think about how I didn't understand them, about how they whizzed through my young mind. And I've been thinking lately about the Phoenix. The myth of the Phoenix has its roots in Arabic mythology and is a story about death and resurrection. Most commonly, we think of the Phoenix as a bird that rises out of the ashes in an act of self-regeneration. There is more to the story. It is a story about how children participate in the resurrection of their parents.

In most versions of the surviving myth, the Phoenix is a bird of great beauty, a magnificent creature, possibly resembling an eagle, but much larger and brilliantly colored in red and gold plumage. Herodotus tells us that when the parent Phoenix dies, the child must provide for its mythic burial. To accomplish this, the young Phoenix gathers myrrh and creates an enormous egg, large enough to carry the dead parent. It scrapes out the inside of the egg, places the dead parent inside, seals it up, and carries it off to Egypt, the sanctuary of the sun, which dies each night and returns each morning.

Although Herodotus does not say it, the act of putting the dead parent in an egg, which is the source of new life, is clear. From the egg, and like the sun, the parent will find rebirth and new life. The resonance of the myth with our own beliefs of saving our dead is clear.

Herodotus says he doesn't believe the story of the Phoenix. I don't believe it literally, but I believe it's a true story about the power of love for one's father, the respect of carrying the dead father to the land of the sun, and the redemption of the parent through the love of the child. That devotion reaches way down inside me and grabs hold. I can't explain why. I just know that the image of the Phoenix with the father is powerful and archetypal.

I feel that dedication turning to my sons as well. It has taken a while for me to outgrow the memories of raising sons through the teen years, through the years of outrageous auto insurance, the years of them sneaking out in the middle of the night and talking back and claiming adults know nothing. Those were hard times—for them and for me—and I find myself still amazed that four competent sons, sons for whom I had little hope even five or ten years ago, are actually amounting to something, that they do things I can't do, that they know things I don't know.

Turning my heart to my sons has come with no small dose of humility, and I find humility a rotten fish to swallow. Especially when Sam, the youngest, delivers it on a silver platter.

Sam needed a dental examination before his mission. The dentist recommended that he have his wisdom teeth extracted. Sam was moaning about how he didn't want his wisdom teeth extracted. He didn't want the pain and inconvenience of the ordeal. It was just a few days before Christmas, and he was afraid some oral surgeon would ruin his seasonal cheer. Poor baby. I kept his upper lip stiff for him, offering encouragement like, "Sam, when your mom had her wisdom teeth out, she slept that afternoon, and after that she was fine. This is not going to spoil Christmas, so get a grip on yourself." He was not convinced. Like a drill sergeant, I marched him to the surgeon's office, urging him to keep pace and face the world with courage. I have many lessons in courage to teach my sons, and I use them liberally.

The date was December 18. We scheduled his extractions for December 22. Sam pouted, I preached. This was going to happen, no doubt about it.

I had a dental exam with our dentist the next day, December 19. Poking around with his little prod, noting that everything looked just fine, Dr. Adams suddenly grunted. Actually, it was a combined grunt and a whistle. Then he said, "Oh, man. Oh, man oh man. Can't you feel that?"

I could feel him tugging at some tooth at the rear of my mouth, but I couldn't feel any pain. "I've got this wire stuck all the way through your wisdom tooth," he said. "You should be feeling some serious pain."

Did he want me in pain? I thought of my childhood dentist, who once drilled all the way through a molar without giving me a painkiller. Those were the days of the Wild West, when men were men and dentists were dentists. I felt nothing. Actually, I felt slightly nauseated. I had avoided wisdom tooth extraction for thirty-five years. The first guy who wanted to pull them was a dentist known to some as the Merry Butcher. When I went for a routine checkup once, he gleefully spotted my wisdom teeth.

"Those need to come out," he said. "You might as well have it done while it's free with your student insurance."

I shuddered, remembered all too clearly stories of my friends' extractions at his hands, said I'd think it over, and never spoke to him again. Over the years other dentists, respectable dentists, urged extraction. It needed to be done before the teeth went bad, they said, before they pressured my other teeth into misalignment, they said, before I got to an age when pulling wisdom teeth involves greater risk and more pain. I never asked what the risk or the pain was. I always nodded, told them I'd think it over, and ignored the advice.

Now, on this fateful December day, my family dentist, whom I respect and trust, was tugging at a crater in my wisdom tooth and whistling. I've never liked hearing a dentist whistle.

"You've got two choices," he said. "I can fill that tooth for you, try to extend its life, or you can have it pulled. Actually," he said, as he examined the other three wisdom teeth, "you really need to get all of them pulled. It's high time. To be honest, you don't have two choices. The hole in that tooth goes all the way through, and filling it is just putting off the inevitable." He flipped through my chart. "Yeah, oh yeah. Let's see. Birth year 1939. You're coming up on sixty. You're way past time."

He finished my checkup and turned me loose. I felt like cattle I had seen jumping up and running around after they'd been branded. I took a card for the same oral surgeon I had visited with Sam just the day before. On the drive home, I thought about how I would tell Louise. How could I do it so that I wouldn't get the full force of her scorn? There were no words. Alas, poor Tom. On the way I stopped at the oral surgeon's office.

The same cheerful receptionist greeted me. "Oh, hello, Mr. Plummer. What can we do for you?" There's something about pretty, cheerful receptionists in an oral surgeon's office that turns my stomach.

She checked the appointment schedule. "Oh, this is cute," she said. "We can book you and Sam at the same time."

Really cute. Peachy. Peachy keen.

I walked into the house. Unlike most days, I didn't call out a cheerful "hello" to Louise.

"Tom? Is that you?" She was in her study finishing up grades from the end of the semester.

"Yeah," I said.

"What's wrong?" she asked. Louise has always had this uncanny ability to know from a great distance when something is wrong with me. It seems to come through the air to her. I don't need to say more than one word, I don't need to say any words at all, and she knows if follow-up is in order. It's a totally unsettling fact of my marriage that I have absolutely no way of keeping a secret.

"I'm having my wisdom teeth pulled on December 22—the same time as Sam."

A long, loud, very long and very loud belly laugh rolled down the stairs and landed on my head.

"It's not that funny," I said.

"Oh, it's very funny," she said. "You've been avoiding this for years, and now you'll do it with Sam. It'll be a bonding experience, a father-son outing. Didn't I hear you telling Sam to get a grip on himself?"

I was not interested in a bonding experience. Not with Sam under these conditions, and certainly not with his surgeon.

"And is Dr. Rasband going to do the extraction?"

"Yes."

"Oh, goody," she said. Louise has a history with Dr. Rasband. When our son Ed needed surgery to correct an overbite, Dr. Rasband was the man for the job. He'd done a lot of this type of surgery, which involves breaking the jawbone near the joint and sliding the jaw forward to align the upper and lower teeth. It's a nasty surgery, and when it's over, it's not over. Ed had to have his jaw wired shut for eight weeks while it healed. His diet consisted of liquids or solids turned into liquids. Liquid Big Macs and fries, that sort of thing. The dentist gave him a pair of wire cutters in case he began to choke, so that in an emergency he could clip the wires holding his jaw shut.

Being the son of nervous parents, Ed is a nervous type, and he was extra nervous about Dr. Rasband, because in an effort to assure Ed that everything was all right, the good doctor had a habit of patting Ed on the leg. This made Ed quite jittery.

Louise's response was to predict the future. "I'll prophesy for you, Ed. You'll be on the table, the anesthesia will be numbing you to sleep, and just before you go out, Dr. Rasband will lean over and kiss you on the lips."

All of this must have flashed through her mind as I announced that Dr. Rasband would perform my surgery. Even if she were to deny it, I know this passed through her mind. And more. The fact that I'd been so condescending toward Sam, so paternalistic, assuring him that having his wisdom teeth extracted was no big deal, that Dr. Rasband was a fine surgeon, was a pleasure all its own.

When the day came, Sam went first. I followed. Louise waited for us and took us home, two guys drunk on whatever anesthesia they administered. By midafternoon, Sam was up and about. I was flat on my back. Sam had no pain. I had excruciating pain. By evening, Sam went out with his friends. I went to bed. By morning, Sam could barely remember the extractions. I had the onset of dry socket, which eventually led to several packings at the hands of kindly Dr. Rasband. Then came an infection, followed by antibiotics and then stronger antibiotics.

In the movie *Guess Who's Coming to Dinner,* the daughter of an upscale, white, Anglo-Saxon, Protestant family is bringing her date, Sidney Poitier, home to meet her folks. The parents have gone berserk that their daughter is even considering an interracial relationship. A family friend teases the father, "It's a terrible thing when an old liberal comes face to face with his principles." I have thought of that line many times since my wisdom teeth bestowed so much wisdom on my head. Sometimes I wonder where this paternalistic arrogance of mine comes from. I certainly despise it in others. I don't care for doctors, store clerks, and bus drivers who talk down to me. I don't care for nursing homes where caregivers talk baby-talk to old people. I really don't care for parents who yell at their kids and say, "If you do that again, I'm gonna smack you."

Paternalism of that kind doesn't come from my dad. He held me when I was afraid. He's the model of a father I struggle to be, try to remember to be, and too often forget. I hope I'm getting a little closer to that model. I'm often reminded of it now. When I drink a little cold water and pain shoots up through my ex-wisdom teeth and into my head, I remember that kindness to sons is better than arrogance. My heart turns to my children in the very moment it is turning to my father.

When Sam arrived home from his mission, he needed

toiletries—toothbrush, toothpaste, shampoo, and, he told me, a Gillette Mach 3 razor. I had never heard of a Mach 3 razor. My shaving instrument of choice is a little disposable BIC razor with a white plastic handle and head and a bright yellow blade guard that you throw away on first use. I've been using BIC razors since 1960-something, and found them quite satisfactory. About once a year I buy another bag of ten, and that keeps me just fine.

But Sam is a man of the modern age, and now an adult, so I didn't grill and torture him as I might have in his younger years. I dutifully looked for a Mach 3 razor, which I wouldn't normally shop for any more than I'd shop for an F-16. I found one on the shelf at Albertson's in a theft-proof plastic box. I knew I was out of my league as soon as I saw it. The Mach 3 Shaving System, as it is called, is a name for the space age, a name for the electronic age, a name for an age that I feel myself groping to understand in the way a drowning man might grope for a branch or rock. Not only did it cost as much as a four-year supply of my BIC razors, its very design spoke of a new generation of shavers, mounted in its black and silver case, with its black and silver striped handle and removable, triple-blade head, honed as finely as any surgical tool. It has a dangerous Darth-Vader look that says "old men can get hurt using this."

While Louise and Sam were sleeping the next morning, I tiptoed into the bathroom to have a closer look at it. I was handling it cautiously, but in an unfocused moment I pushed a little button on the handle. The head popped off. I was afraid I wouldn't be able to get it back on, and I was wondering how I would explain to Sam that I had been playing with his razor and couldn't put it back together again. Humpty Dumpty came to mind. But I finally managed to reassemble it, and the fact that I ever played with it or touched it remains my little secret.

I've been wondering about my obsession with Sam's Mach 3 shaver. Of course it's a guy thing. But it's more than that. For men, razors and shaving are symbolic. Shaving has a place in the scriptures. Joseph shaved before he went to see Pharaoh. Samson knew that if his head was shaved, he would lose his strength. The Levite priests in Ezekiel were told not to shave their heads. The Lamanites in the Book of Mormon shaved their heads to symbolize their savagery.

Having facial hair means you're a man. Shaving is one of the first things a young man does to affirm that he is coming of age. My father taught me to shave by doing the first job on me himself, showing me how to lather, how to drag that bulky old 1950s razor with its Gillette blue blade gently across my face. When I went off to the army in 1958 for basic training, I bought my first razor and quit using the one I shared with my dad. It was a moment of manhood. Men don't talk much about these things. I don't know for sure if we fear putting the blade to our face or if we're afraid of growing up. I think we know, at some subconscious level, that we are entering a new and dangerous time of our lives. The shaving instrument symbolizes that danger, but we don't let ourselves think much about it.

Forty-five years ago I was in the basement of the family home with my father rummaging around through some drawers that no one had looked in for a long time. Dad, who was a little younger than I am now, saw an old, thin black box that he opened with trembling fingers. The only other time I had seen my father's hands tremble was when he caught a five-pound rainbow trout on the Green River. Inside the box was an old, straight-edged razor. He pulled it out, saying over and over, "Look, Tom, it's my dad's old razor. It's my dad's old razor."

At the time I didn't see the importance that he obviously saw, didn't feel the symbolic weight that he felt. But I do now. Recently, when my sister and I were cleaning out my mother's house, I came upon that razor again. "I want that," I said.

She looked a little puzzled, shrugged her shoulders, and said, "It's yours."

I have kept it in a special box.

My colleague Leslie Norris has written a story called "Shaving," in which a young man of seventeen has to shave his dying father. The story illustrates how shaving becomes a way for the mantle of authority to pass from father to son:

> Barry cradled his father's head in the crook of his left arm, so that the man could tilt back his head, exposing the throat. He brushed fresh lather under the chin and into the hollows alongside the stretched tendons. His father's throat was fleshless and vulnerable, his head was

a hard weight on the boy's arm. Barry was filled with unreasoning protective love. He lifted the razor and began to shave.

"You don't have to worry," he said. "Not at all. Not about anything."

[The father] leaned his head tiredly against the boy's shoulder. He was without strength, his face was cold and smooth. He had let go all his authority, handed it over. He lay back on his pillow, knowing his weakness and his mortality, and looked at his son with wonder, with a curious humble pride.

"I won't worry then," he said. "About anything." (*The Girl from Cardigan* [Layton, UT: Gibbs Smith, 1988], 94–95)

What struck me so forcibly in reading this story again, a thought brought on by Sam's razor, is that the father teaches the son to shave, but the son must shave the dying father and thereby assume his authority. It's a patriarchal ritual; it's a ritual as old as humankind.

I never felt the nearness of this ritual more forcibly than when Sam stepped into the airport, back from his mission in the Philippines. One of my students asked me if he had changed. "He's a man. He left a boy and came home a man," I said. A friend said the other day that he felt slightly cheated that he could not watch that transformation in his missionary son firsthand. I don't know if it's possible for the father to watch. I think it may be necessary for the son to leave, change, and return.

My biggest struggle has been to avoid treating Sam as a boy, to treat him as the man he has become. In order to get my struggle aboveboard, I told him that I knew he'd been doing important things, leading missionaries, baptizing people, being guided by the Spirit. I didn't want to treat him any more as I had in the past, I said, I knew he had become a man. "I don't want to treat you like a baby," I said.

"Sometimes I like being a baby," he said, and laid his head on Louise's shoulder.

It was an endearing moment, but I can see the change, and I can feel it. There's a photograph of me with Dennis Garff and Richard van Wagenen on the steps to the Cambridge Ward just after Richard had blessed his son Michael in fast and testimony meeting. The three of us are wearing navy blue suits, white shirts, and red ties. We are as radiant and filled with hope as three young men could possibly be. Richard holds his son proudly, with Dennis and me standing on either side. It is the spring of 1967.

Although I had already performed the ritual of shaving my dying father in his hospital bed three years before that picture was taken, I could not foresee in 1967 the homecoming thirty-four years later of my youngest son from the Philippines, a son as tall and radiant as we were that day, a son who could someday be shaving me.

Like the father in my colleague's story, I know I'm in good hands, and I won't worry. It's a great comfort, as I imagine my ritual shaving, to have four fine sons, four sons to whom I can entrust my exposed throat, four sons in whom I can feel a "curious humble pride."

In honor of Sam's manhood, I have passed the razor on to him. I have passed on the razor his Great-Grandfather Plummer once used, the razor his Grandfather Plummer once held with shaking hands in memory of his father, the razor he may someday pass on to his son to commemorate his manhood.

Malachi was right. The hearts of the fathers turn to their children. The hearts of the children turn to their fathers.

ABOUT THE AUTHOR

Tom Plummer received master's and Ph.D. degrees from Harvard University and is a professor of German language and literature at Brigham Young University. His previous books include *Eating Chocolates and Dancing in the Kitchen,* an award-winning collection of sketches about marriage and family; *Don't Bite Me, I'm Santa Claus;* and *Second Wind: Variations on a Theme of Growing Older.* He and his wife, Louise, have been married for more than thirty-five years. They have four sons and seven grandchildren.

Also by Tom Plummer:

EATING CHOCOLATES AND DANCING IN THE KITCHEN
Sketches of Marriage and Family

DON'T BITE ME, I'M SANTA CLAUS

SECOND WIND Variations on a Theme of Growing Older

Excerpted from SECOND WIND: Variations on a Theme of Growing Older

STEADY OR NOT, HERE I COME

Several months ago when Louise and I were at the mall, I looked down and saw that I was wearing my house slippers. I recalled an uncle who always wore his house slippers when he came to visit, and I thought he was downright odd. My mother always said of such people, "He's kinda differ'nt, don'cha think?" . . .

I made the mistake of pointing out my gaffe to Louise. "Look," I said, "I'm wearing my house slippers." She broke into gales of laughter. She stood in the open mall, her hand on her forehead, her mouth wide open, hee-hawing.

"What's so funny about that?" I wanted to know.

This brought even harder laughing. "You're turning into an old man," she said. "I can't wait to tell our friends that you've started wearing your house slippers to the mall."

Not long afterward, when Louise was in New York and I was no longer under her watchful eye, our friends Al and

Ginny invited me to go to dinner. It might have been a this-guy-is-alone-and-needs-some-company-before-he-goes-nuts consolation prize. Friends have observed that I become loony when left alone for more than twenty-four hours; they try to watch out for me. I readily accepted their invitation and arrived at their house at the appointed hour. I had no sooner entered their front hall than I looked down and saw that I was again wearing my house slippers.

"I've forgotten something," I said. "I'll be right back." I jumped in the car, raced home, put on real shoes, and sped back to Al and Ginny's.

"Ready," I said. "Let's go."

"What was that all about?" Al wanted to know.

"I was wearing my house slippers," I said. "I had to put on street shoes."

"We wouldn't care if you wore your house slippers to a restaurant," Ginny said.

"You don't understand," I said. "I really have to wear shoes. If Louise ever found out I'd worn my house slippers to a restaurant, I'd never hear the end of it."

When Louise came home from New York, we again went out to eat with Al and Ginny.

"Did you know," Al said to Louise over bisque at the Capitol Café, "that Tom wore his house slippers to dinner the other night?"

I suppose wearing house slippers in public is a sign of absentmindedness in aging. It may even signify that I'm just a bit "differ'nt." But "differ'nt" from what? I certainly hope "differ'nt" from the teenagers I see around town. . . . "Differ'nt," in my late-middle-aged view, is Dr. Martens shoes, which are the rage among younger people. For those lucky enough to have finished raising their children more than ten years ago, let me explain that Dr. Martens are among the ugliest footwear ever to hit the planet. Their hallmark, in a word, is bulk. Morbid obesity. They are so robust that the manufacturer claims in one promo, "While in Bosnia, BBC correspondent Kate Adie came under attack, and two pieces of shrapnel pierced her foot. She says that her Dr. Martens boots saved her foot by absorbing most of the shock from the blast." But to say that the single quality of this footwear is mass is to oversimplify the matter and widens the chasm between me and the younger generation. . . .

So Dr. Martens are for young folks, and house slippers are for old guys. I rather like wearing my house slippers. They have thin, inconspicuous soles, suede tops with, I admit, a large stitch down the middle on top, and comfortable, fake-sheepskin lining. They don't cry out for attention, they keep my feet warm, and I can walk for long distances without becoming dehydrated. Best of all, they're absolutely non-violent: I couldn't kick anyone's shins without hurting myself.

Louise says that I've got it wrong, that Dr. Martens are for young folks and house slippers are for old geezers who can't remember to put on their shoes. Wearing house slippers in public is a sign of instability. Her thinking comes close to that of Jean Paul when he wrote, "The young man is deliberately odd and prides himself on it, the old man is unintentionally so, and it mortifies him."

Close, but no truffle. My house slippers do not mortify me. They mortify Louise. I find Goethe's thinking more in line with my feelings on the subject: "It does not become a man of years to follow the fashion, either in his thinking or his dress." Goethe was a classy guy. I'll take his word for it. I'm not going to follow the fashion of the young folks, that's for sure. As for my thinking, maybe I am a little wobbly in the head, but steady or not, here I come.